Practice Book

6

Numeracy Focus

Practice Book

6

Written by Len Frobisher
Edited by Sheila Ebbutt and Mike Askew

RIGBY

Rigby
Halley Court, Jordan Hill, Oxford, OX2 8EJ
a division of Reed Educational and Professional Publishing Ltd

Rigby is a registered trademark of Reed Educational and Professional Publishing Ltd

OXFORD MELBOURNE AUCKLAND
JOHANNESBURG BLANTYRE GABORONE
IBADAN PORTSMOUTH (NH) CHICAGO

Written by Len Frobisher
Edited by Sheila Ebbutt and Mike Askew

First published 2000

05 04 03 02 01 00
10 9 8 7 6 5 4 3 2 1

ISBN 0 435 21788 7

Typeset by DP Press
Illustrated by DP Press and Peters and Zebransky
Printed by Edelvives, Zaragosa, Spain

Introduction

Children need two different kinds of practice to consolidate their mathematics learning:

- guided practice (teacher-led support to help with new ideas)
- independent practice (to consolidate knowledge and skills already learned).

To help distinguish between these types of practice, **Numeracy Focus** provides its practice resources in separate books. This *Practice Book* provides the opportunity for independent practice.

Once children have learned the mathematics, they need time for independent practice so they can consolidate their ideas and their skills become fluent. The *Practice Book* is designed for children to have short periods of focused practice with an emphasis on speed as well as accuracy.

The exercises in the *Practice Book* provide material for two sessions of practice a week, each lasting about 10 to 15 minutes. The content of each session is derived from material taught in the *Teaching and Learning File* during the previous 4-6 weeks. This allows time for children to consolidate their learning and to be ready to practise it with some fluency. To assist this, and promote confidence, the questions are set at a slightly easier level than the material actually taught.

The content of the *Practice Book* pages is mixed, drawing on the range of skills and knowledge children build on during the year. There is an emphasis on numerical skills, together with a smaller range of questions on measures, shape and space, and data handling. The first exercise for each session consists of quick calculation questions. The last question is generally more open-ended, offering children scope to apply their mathematics knowledge more flexibly.

Attached to some of the exercises is a hint box. Hint boxes contain tips and examples to help children work out answers.

The material is presented in a range of formats, which will have been introduced to children during the lessons and in the accompanying activities in the *Teaching and Learning File*. It is important that children become used to different ways of presenting mathematics exercises and problems so that they learn the skills of extracting information and making sense of written tasks. Children will have learned specific mathematical vocabulary during mathematics lessons and they should understand and know how to use it.

Children record their answers to *Practice Book* questions in an exercise book. In order to set out their work clearly and to help with the drawing of tables and charts, this book should be the standard mathematics exercise book bound with squared paper. As the *Practice Book* is designed for children to practise aspects of mathematics they are more confident with, they can be encouraged to pay more attention to the setting out of their work. This exercise book can offer a more 'public' presentation of their mathematics, and children should be encouraged to work clearly, neatly and systematically.

Practice 1a

1 Copy these and complete them.

1	39 × 10 = ____	2	9 × 8 = ____	3	340 − 190 = ____
4	What is 6^2?	5	250 + 750 = ____	6	402 − 298 = ____
7	529 + 97 = ____	8	413 + 140 = ____	9	Half of 84

2

1 How long does it take the bus to get from Adle to the City?

2 Carrie arrives at Leek at 08:17. What time is the next bus due to arrive at Leek?

3 Harry wants to get to the City at 12:10. What time should he catch the bus from Adle?

Bus times

Adle	06:15	every 20	10:15	every 30	14:15
Leek	06:27	minutes	10:27	minutes	14:27
City	06:40		10:40		14:40

3 Copy the grid and fill in the missing numbers.

litres	2	7		1·5		$\frac{1}{10}$	6·5	
millilitres	2000		4000		3500			10

4

1 A jug contains 655 ml of water. Asad pours out 250 ml. How much is left in the jug?

2 A bucket holds $5\frac{1}{2}$ litres. A dog bath is filled using 8 bucketfuls of water. How many litres of water are in the bath?

3 A full bottle of cough medicine contains 125 ml. How many 5 ml spoonfuls can be made from a full bottle?

5 Copy these three multiplications. Choose three different pairs of numbers from the box to complete the multiplications.

12 = ☐ × ☐ 12 = ☐ × ☐ 12 = ☐ × ☐

Do this again for the numbers 18, 28 and 42.

14 6 28 7 3 18 1 12 2 9 42 21 4

Practice 1b

1 Copy these and write the missing numbers.

1	6 times ☐ = 54	2	40 + ☐ + 50 = 190	3	☐ − 52 = 48
4	☐ ÷ 6 = 7	5	463 + ☐ = 500	6	☐ × 10 = 470
7	503 − ☐ = 205	8	☐ − 3·7 = 2·4	9	300 × ☐ = 2400

2

1 Explain how to find the number of days in any number of weeks.

2 Describe how to calculate the area of a square.

3 Explain how to find the double of any number.

4 Describe how to calculate the number of whole pounds in any number of pence.

3 Show each of these times using 24-hour notation.

1 → 09:50

1 10 minutes to 10 in the morning

2 A quarter past 2 in the afternoon

3 6:45 a.m.

4 3:30 p.m.

5 1 minute after midnight

4 Copy the decimal addition.

1·6 + 1·5 = 3·1

☐·6 + ☐·5

Choose a digit from the oval. Use it twice to complete the addition.
Work out the answer.

Do this with all five digits.

1 5 4 3 7

5 Copy these and write the signs (+, −, × or ÷) that are hiding behind the stars.

1	54 ☆ 9 = 486	2	54 ☆ 9 = 45	3	54 ☆ 9 = 6
4	56 ☆ 14 = 42	5	56 ☆ 14 = 784	6	56 ☆ 14 = 70

Practice 2a

1 Copy these and complete them.

1 280 – 140 = ____
2 30 + 90 + 70 = ____
3 435 + 47 = ____
4 7·2 – 4·8 = ____
5 600 + 400 + 700 = ____
6 450 × 100 = ____
7 Share 48 between 2
8 4017 + 996 = ____
9 25 × 16 = ____

2 Copy the statements. Choose numbers from the box to make the statements correct.

1 year = 365 days

1 1 year = ☐ days
2 1 century = ☐ years
3 1 hour = ☐ minutes
4 1 year = ☐ weeks
5 1 day = ☐ hours
6 1 minute = ☐ seconds

364 1 10 42 365 60 24 50 366 25 52 100

3 Choose three numbers from the grid with a sum of 1000.

511 + 71 + 418 = 1000

166	230	2
71	418	164
323	670	511

Do this for three sets of numbers.

4 Choose a number from each circle to complete the statement.

☐ litres = ☐ millilitres

7, 1·5, 3, 6, 0·3, 2·7

2700, 6000, 300, 700, 3000, 1500

Do this for five amounts of litres.

5 Write four different things you know about odd numbers.

Practice 2b

1 Copy these and write the missing numbers.

1	□ + 300 = 826	2	□ + 39 = 100	3	10% of □ = 9 km
4	□ + 150 = 429	5	□ × 5 = 1·5	6	□ × 6 = 198
7	520 − □ = 330	8	□ + 36 = 352	9	□ × 400 = 20 000

2

1 

1 pint

2 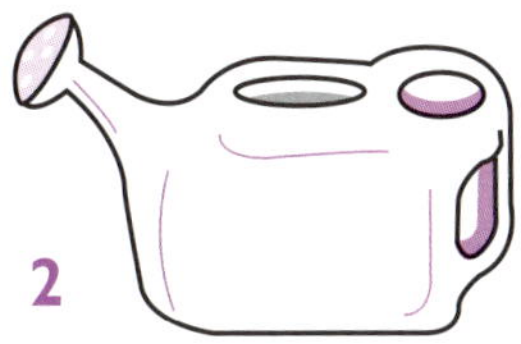

2 gallons

3 

2 pints

4 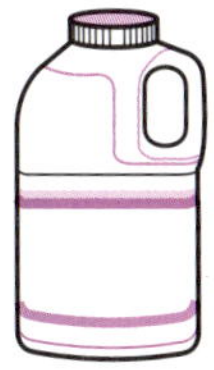

1 gallon

Choose quantities from the box to write the approximate capacity of the containers.

5 litres	2 litres	1 litre	400 millilitres	10 litres	500 millilitres

3 Copy the addition and the subtraction.

Use the eight digits from the circle to complete both calculations.

Work out the answers.

238 + 91 = 329
456 − 71 = 385

□□□ + □1 = □

□□□ − □1 = □

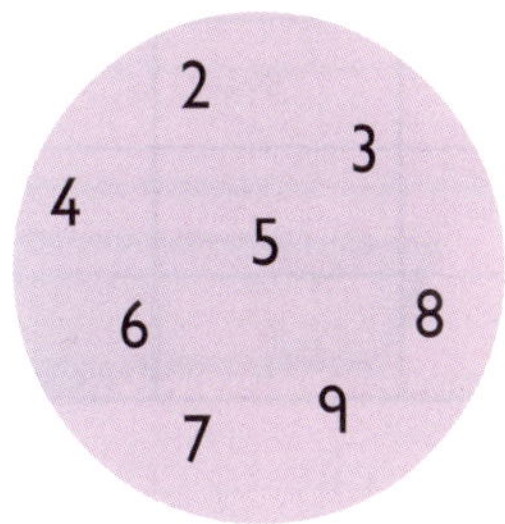

Do this five times.

4 Estimate:

1 the number of hours in one year

2 the number of breaths you take in one day

3 the time it takes you to walk one mile

4 the time you sleep in one month.

5 Write four different things you know about even numbers.

Practice 3a

1

Copy these and complete them.

1	From 80 take 27	2	1·6 + 1·5 = ____	3	4001 – 3997 = ____
4	Total 53 and 58	5	56 ÷ 8 = ____	6	100 – 43 = ____
7	600 ÷ 10 = ____	8	537 + 600 = ____	9	$\frac{1}{5}$ of £100

2

Copy and complete these statements using the words 'odd' or 'even'.

1 The sum of two odd numbers is never ______________ .

2 The difference between two odd numbers is always ______________ .

3 The sum of three odd numbers is always ______________ .

4 The sum of an even and an odd number is never ______________ .

3

1 Explain how to find the number of metres in any number of kilometres.

2 Describe how to calculate the area of a rectangle.

3 Explain how to find a half of any even number.

4 Describe how to calculate the number of pence in any number of 50p coins.

4

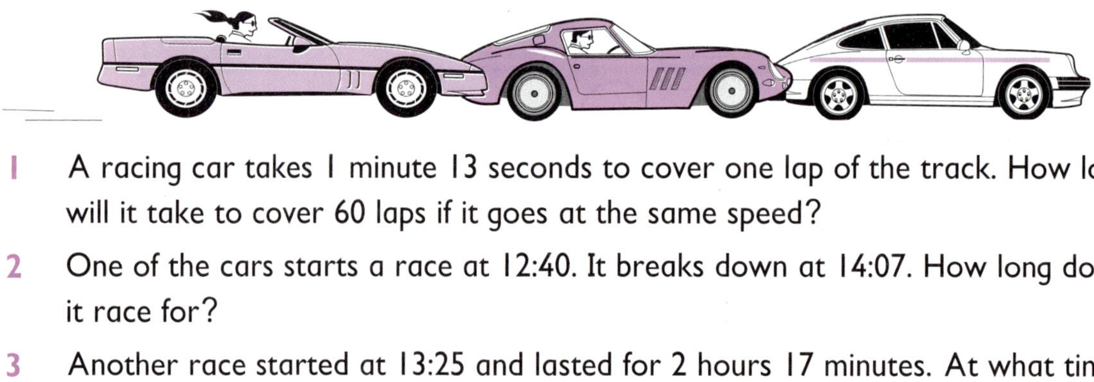

1 A racing car takes 1 minute 13 seconds to cover one lap of the track. How long will it take to cover 60 laps if it goes at the same speed?

2 One of the cars starts a race at 12:40. It breaks down at 14:07. How long does it race for?

3 Another race started at 13:25 and lasted for 2 hours 17 minutes. At what time did the race end?

5

Copy the multiplication four times.
Find four different pairs of 2-digit numbers whose product is 864.

[2][4] × [3][6] = 864

[ ][ ] × [ ][ ] = 864

Practice 3b

1 Copy these and write the missing numbers.

1	4·2 + ☐ = 5	2	618 + ☐ = 713	3	280 × ☐ = 2800
4	36 divided by ☐ = 6	5	☐ + 2·6 = 5·1	6	2200 ÷ ☐ = 220
7	☐ + 2300 = 4600	8	200 + 400 + ☐ = 1200	9	☐ − 1999 = 7

2

1. A factory makes 1000 litres of cough medicine each hour. How many 125 millilitre bottles will 1000 litres make?
2. The sauce in a full bottle weighs 425 grams. At a meal a family uses 49 grams of the sauce. What is the weight of the sauce left in the bottle?
3. The winner of a long jump competition leaps 5·30 metres. He wins by 90 centimetres. How far did the second placed jumper leap?

3 Copy the statement. Choose a number from each oval to complete the statement.

☐ millilitres = ☐ litres

300, 3000, 330, 3300

3, 0·33, 0·3, 3·3

Do all this for all four amounts of millilitres.

4 Copy the diagrams. Find different pairs of factors to complete the diagrams.

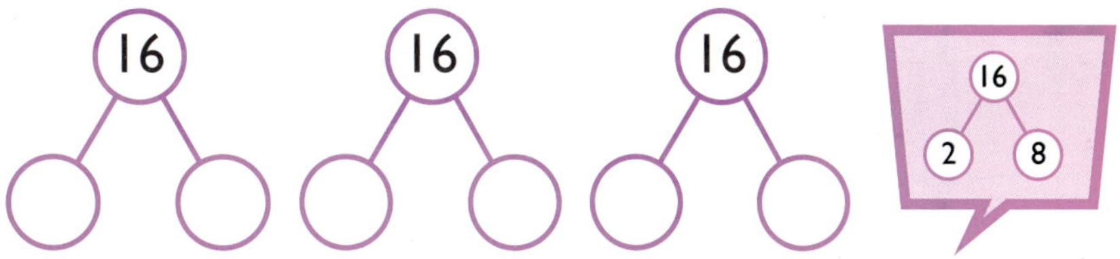

Repeat for the numbers 24, 32 and 45.

5 How many 1 × 1, 2 × 2 and 3 × 3 squares can you count in the 4 × 4 square? There are more than 16.

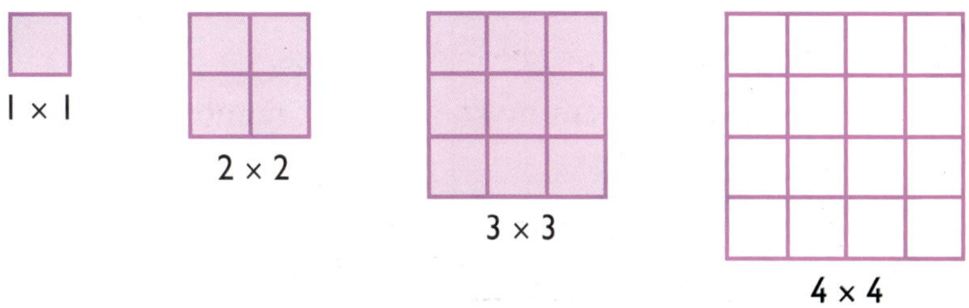

Practice 4a

1 Copy these and complete them.

1	2·7 + 2·8 = ____	2	270 + 180 = ____	3	Double 39
4	7200 ÷ 100 = ____	5	0·2 + 0·8 = ____	6	3·8 + 2·3 = ____
7	654 − 98 = ____	8	0·2 × 7 = ____	9	78 ÷ 6 = ____

2 Copy the addition and the subtraction. Choose any four digits to complete the calculations. Work out the answers.

[3][5][ ] + [1][9][ ] = [ ]

[7][0][ ] − [4][9][ ] = [ ]

[3][5][7] + [1][9][2] = 549

[7][0][8] − [4][9][1] = 217

Do this for four different sets of digits.

3 Choose two numbers from the oval. Find their product. Using factors may help you.

Do this for five pairs of numbers.

15 16 14 18 12

16 × 12 = 16 × 2 × 2 × 3 = 32 × 2 × 3 = 64 × 3 = 192

4 Copy and complete these subtractions.

1	£4.59 − £2.83 = £[ ]	2	36·5 km − 4·7 km = [ ] km
3	5·61 g − 1·25 g = [ ] g	4	£6.17 − £1.89 = £[ ]
5	18·5 ml − 3·8 ml = [ ] ml	6	97·2 kg − 49·5 kg = [ ] kg

5 Copy these divisions. Complete the divisions by choosing any digits, apart from 1, so that the answers are whole numbers.

1	[5][ ] ÷ [ ] = [ ]	2	[6][ ] ÷ [ ] = [ ]
3	[7][ ] ÷ [ ] = [ ]	4	[8][ ] ÷ [ ] = [ ]

Repeat three times for each division.

Practice 4b

1 Copy these and write the missing numbers.

1	□ + 989 = 4107	2	□ × 2 = 450	3	476 − □ = 156
4	0·3 + □ = 1	5	1 − □ = 0·2	6	0·4 × □ = 1·2
7	72 ÷ □ = 12	8	□ + 1·6 = 4·5	9	4193 − □ = 3693

2 For each set of three numbers write two additions and two subtractions.

1. 111, 222 and 333
2. 362, 157 and 519
3. 226, 701 and 475
4. 589, 291 and 298

3 Copy the four statements. For each statement write three examples.

1. The sum of an odd and an even number is odd.
2. The difference between an odd and an even number is odd.
3. The sum of three even numbers is even.
4. The difference between two odd numbers is even.

4 Copy and complete these additions.

1	£5.08 + £3.76 = £□	2	29·8 km + 6·7 km = □ km
3	7·53 kg + 2·62 kg = □ kg	4	£3.94 + £4.06 = £□
5	14·8 m + 7·6 m = □ m	6	35·8 ml + 17·9 ml = □ ml

5 Copy the multiplication grids. Write the numbers from 2 to 10 twice each to fill the shaded boxes. Complete the grids.
Do it again a different way.

×	2	3	4
5			
6			
7			

×	8	9	10
2			
3			
4			

×	5	6	7
8			
9			
10			

×			

×			

×			

Practice 5a

1 Copy these and complete them.

1	2728 − 800 = ____	2	25% of 60 kg	3	$\frac{1}{10}$ of £30
4	30 × 600 = ____	5	8 times 7	6	29 + 29 = ____
7	3400 ÷ 100 = ____	8	150 + 460 = ____	9	1 − 0·6 = ____

2
1 I think of a number and divide it by 12. The answer is 60. What was my number?
2 There are 56 biscuits in a tin. How many biscuits are there in a box of 20 tins?
3 A cinema has 235 seats. At the start of a film 169 seats are empty. How many people are in the cinema?

3 Copy the addition and subtraction grids and complete them.

+	8		
	17		
6		9	13
5			

−	15		19
	3		
8			
	11	8	

+			
6	17		
9			17
17		31	

−	20		30
8		32	
	9		
			15

4 Write two different numbers which match each statement.
1 A number with 4 hundreds and 6 thousands.
2 A number with 7 ones and 9 hundred thousands.
3 A number with 8 tens, 3 ten thousands and 4 millions.
4 A number with 0 ones, 5 hundreds, 8 ten thousands and 1 million.

5 Copy the pairs of incomplete numbers. Write any digits to complete the numbers, then find the number which is halfway between each pair.

1	1	5	6			and	1	5	6		
2	2	9	3			and	2	9	3		
3	7	2	0			and	7	2	0		
4	8	4				and	8	4			

Practice 5b

1 Copy these and write the missing numbers.

1	□ + 130 = 310	2	□ × 6 = 42	3	8 × □ = 64
4	□ ÷ 10 = 30	5	7^2 = □	6	342 − □ = 246
7	3·8 + □ = 7·7	8	Double □ = 148	9	390 ÷ □ = 195

2

1 What is the total cost of the three items?

2 Sam buys 4 jars of jam. How much does he pay?

3 Salim pays for 2 mugs of soup with a £5 note. How much change should he get?

4 How many tins of beans can be bought with a £10 note?

3 Copy the additions and complete them.

0·4 + 0·6 = 1

1 □•□ + □•□ = 1

2 □•□ + □•□ = 10

3 □□ + □□ = 100

4 □ 5 0 + □ 5 0 = 1000

Do this three times for each addition.

4 Write down a 5-digit, a 6-digit, a 7-digit and an 8-digit number.

1 Write each of your four numbers in words.

2 What must be added to each number to make one hundred million?

3 What is the total of the four numbers?

4 Find the difference between the largest and the smallest of the numbers.

5 Write four subtractions that have an answer of 12.
Do the same for the answers 13, 14, 15 and 16.

Practice 6a

1 Copy these and complete them.

1	$6123 - 997 =$ ____	2	$325 \times 2 =$ ____	3	$\frac{1}{100}$ of 8000 m
4	$47 \times 5 =$ ____	5	$60 \times 8 =$ ____	6	$756 - 320 =$ ____
7	$470 \div 2 =$ ____	8	$1100 + 1100 =$ ____	9	$500 \times 7 =$ ____

2

1 Copy and complete the diagram. Write about how it helps to find the answer to $\frac{1}{6}$ of £42.

Do the same to find $\frac{1}{6}$ of 78 kg.

2 Copy and complete the diagram. Write about how it helps to find the answer to $\frac{1}{12}$ of £72.

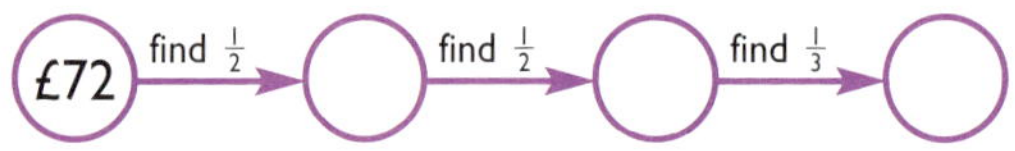

Do the same to find $\frac{1}{12}$ of 156 m.

3 Copy and complete the doubles calculation. Work out the answer. Explain how it works.

double 132 = double [ ][0][0] + double [ ][0] + double [ ] = [ ]

Do the same for double 248, double 372 and double 469.

4 Put each number in turn in your calculator display. Write the numbers in figures.

1 four hundred thousand, one hundred and sixty
2 seven million, twenty-three thousand and seventy
3 forty-one million, thirty thousand and four
4 six hundred and seventy-one thousand

5 Copy the diagram. Write any 4-digit number in the box on the left. Work out the three answers.

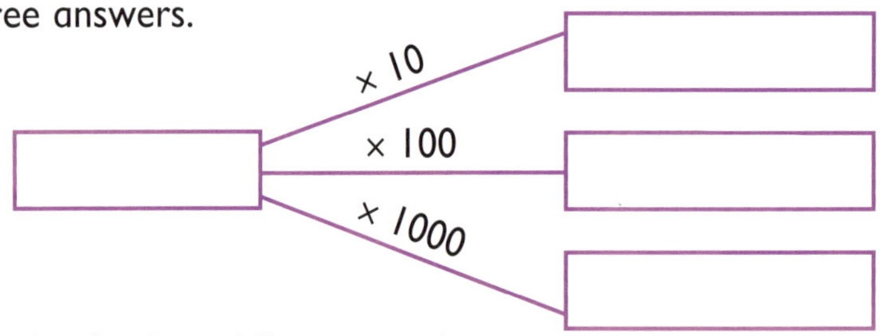

Do this for four different numbers.

Practice 6b

1 Copy these and write the missing numbers.

1 ☐ – 270 = 270
2 Half of ☐ = 370
3 ☐ × 6 = 420
4 $\frac{1}{4}$ of ☐ = 25
5 5900 ÷ ☐ = 59
6 36 ÷ ☐ = 4
7 3004 – ☐ = 6
8 ☐ – 988 = 8243
9 57 + ☐ = 114

2 Copy the calculations. Choose the same two digits from 1 to 9 in the same order to complete each number. Find the answers.

$\frac{1}{2}$ of 268 = 134 $\frac{1}{2}$ of 266 = 133
$\frac{1}{2}$ of 264 = 132 $\frac{1}{2}$ of 262 = 131

$\frac{1}{2}$ of ☐☐8 = ☐ $\frac{1}{2}$ of ☐☐6 = ☐

$\frac{1}{2}$ of ☐☐4 = ☐ $\frac{1}{2}$ of ☐☐2 = ☐

Do this four times.

3 Copy and complete the diagram.

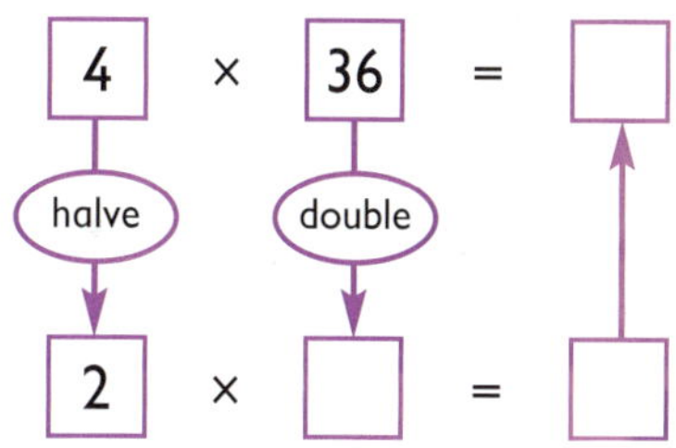

Do the same for the products 6 × 42, 8 × 19 and 20 × 41.

4 Copy and complete the diagram.

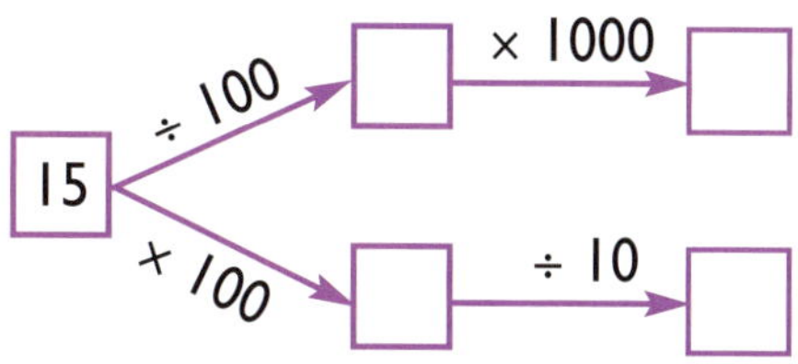

29 50 4 153 270

Do the same for each number in the oval.

What do you notice about each pair of answers? Explain why this is.

5 Copy the doubling calculation. Choose any three digits to complete the 3-digit number. Find its double.

double 417 = 834

double ☐☐☐ = ☐

Do this six times.

Practice 7a

1 Copy these and complete them.

1	$7 \times 10 =$ ____	2	$307 + 288 =$ ____	3	$30 + 60 + 70 =$ ____
4	Half of 84	5	$16 \times 15 =$ ____	6	$400 \div 10 =$ ____
7	$\frac{1}{8}$ of $64 =$ ____	8	Double 65	9	132 divided by 6

2 Copy and complete the grid.

Improper fraction	$\frac{3}{2}$		$\frac{7}{4}$	$\frac{11}{5}$		$\frac{903}{100}$		
Mixed number	$1\frac{1}{2}$	$2\frac{2}{3}$			$4\frac{1}{4}$		$2\frac{5}{8}$	$6\frac{7}{10}$

3 Write these measurements in figures.

1 One kilogram and seventeen hundredths of a kilogram.

2 One metre and six tenths of a metre.

3 Thirty-eight litres and three thousandths of a litre.

4 Four kilometres and ninety-eight thousandths of a kilometre.

4 Copy and complete the diagram.

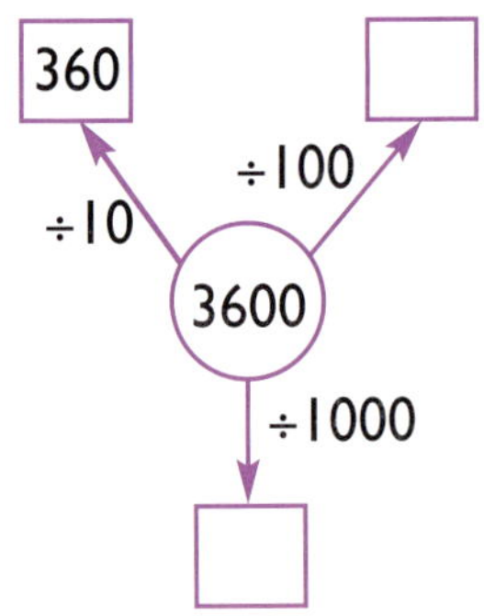

Do the same again, putting these numbers in the circle.

2700	490	27	306	1

5 Copy and complete the calculation by finding a 3-digit number equal to half of a 4-digit number.

Double | 6 | 8 | 0 | = half of | 2 | 7 | 2 | 0 |

Double [ ][ ][ ] = half of [ ][ ][ ][ ]

Repeat with four different pairs of numbers.

Practice 7b

1 Copy these and write the missing numbers.

1 $\square \times 10 = 60$ 2 $\square + 396 = 813$ 3 $\square + 80 + 50 = 150$

4 $\square$ seventeens $= 34$ 5 Double $\square = 82$ 6 Share 96 among $\square = 12$

7 Half of $\square = 85$ 8 $9 \times \square = 81$ 9 $100 \div \square = 4$

2 Copy and complete the calculations. Doubling and halving may help you.

1
$12 \times 10 = \square$
$12 \times 5 = \square$
$12 \times 15 = \square$

2
$36 \times 2 = \square$
$36 \times 4 = \square$
$36 \times 6 = \square$

3
$17 \times 10 = \square$
$17 \times 20 = \square$
$17 \times 30 = \square$

Use the same method to find 152×6 and 136×15.

3 Copy these and write the missing numbers.

1 $\frac{3 \times 2}{4 \times 2} = \frac{\square}{\square}$ 2 $\frac{2 \times 5}{3 \times 5} = \frac{\square}{\square}$ 3 $\frac{3 \times \square}{4 \times \square} = \frac{21}{28}$

4 $\frac{\square \times 4}{\square \times 4} = \frac{12}{20}$ 5 $\frac{\square \times 10}{\square \times 10} = \frac{30}{80}$ 6 $\frac{3 \times \square}{4 \times \square} = \frac{\square}{100}$

4 Copy and complete the diagram.

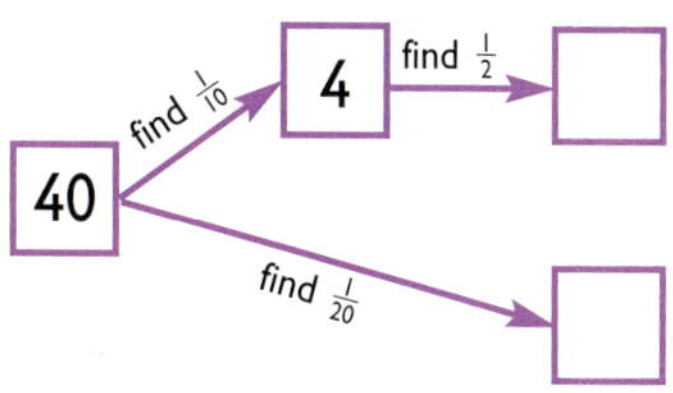

140 60 24 170

Do the same, starting with the numbers in the oval.
What do you notice about each pair of answers? Explain why this is.

5
1 Write down five improper fractions each with a different denominator.
Change each improper fraction to a mixed number.

$\frac{13}{2} = 6\frac{1}{2}$

2 Write down five mixed numbers each with a different denominator.
Change each mixed number to an improper fraction.

$3\frac{3}{4} = \frac{15}{4}$

Practice 8a

1 Copy these and complete them.

1	Double 32	2	Divide 100 into 57	3	5600 ÷ 100 = ____
4	90 + 10 + 50 = ____	5	Half of 180	6	3 ÷ 5 = ____
7	Multiply 15 by 6	8	0·6 × 10 = ____	9	0·75 times 2

2 Lisa draws this diagram to help her find the answer to 24 × 25.

[24] —× 100→ [ ] —halve→ [ ] —halve→ [ ]

Copy and complete Lisa's diagram. What is the answer to 24 × 25?
Explain why Lisa's diagram works.
Do the same to find the answers to 43 × 25, 71 × 25 and 98 × 25.

3

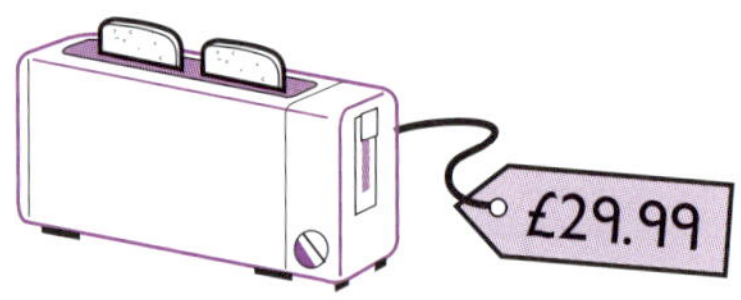

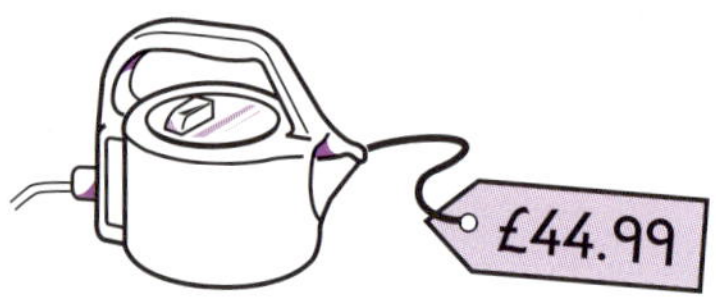

1. Asad buys all three items. How much does he pay?
2. How much change would Daniel get from a £50 note if he bought a coffee-maker?
3. Charlotte pays £79.98 for two of the items. Which two does she buy?

4 Find approximate answers to the multiplications, then work out accurate answers.

1	3841 × 9 = ☐	2	6057 × 6 = ☐	3	4291 × 7 = ☐
4	1888 × 8 = ☐	5	5678 × 4 = ☐	6	4736 × 3 = ☐

5 Copy the grids. Write in each shaded box a number that divides exactly into each of the numbers in the outer boxes.

1

15		6
	(shaded)	18
21	12	

2

	42	28
56	(shaded)	
		35

3

		72
	(shaded)	
36		90

4

	16	96
	(shaded)	
64		32

Write in numbers that belong in the empty outer boxes.

Practice 8b

1 Copy these and write the missing numbers.

1 $\frac{1}{2} = \frac{\square}{8}$ 2 $45 \times \square = 450$ 3 $40 + \square + 60 = 170$

4 Double $\square = 110$ 5 $\square$ divided by $8 = 11$ 6 $\square \times 8 = 64$

7 $\square \times 1000 = 47400$ 8 $56 \div \square = 8$ 9 Half of $\square = 0{\cdot}5$

2 Copy and write in the missing numbers.

1 $\frac{8 \div 2}{16 \div 2} = \frac{\square}{\square}$ 2 $\frac{9 \div 3}{12 \div 3} = \frac{\square}{\square}$ 3 $\frac{70 \div \square}{100 \div \square} = \frac{7}{10}$

4 $\frac{\square \div 5}{\square \div 5} = \frac{4}{5}$ 5 $\frac{\square \div 8}{\square \div 8} = \frac{3}{8}$ 6 $\frac{21 \div \square}{28 \div \square} = \frac{\square}{4}$

3 Copy the multiplication and choose five digits from the box to complete it. Work out the answer.

2	8	9	5	6	7	3	4

$\square\square\square\square \times \square = \square$

Check the answer using an approximation.
Do this for four different sets of numbers.

4 Copy the grid. Match each proportion to its equivalent fraction.

proportion	1 in every 3	2 in every 4	6 in every 8	3 in every 4	3 in every 9
fraction	$\frac{1}{2}$		$\frac{1}{3}$		$\frac{3}{4}$

5 Copy each pair of decimal numbers. Choose two consecutive digits from 0 to 9 to complete a pair.

3·73 and 3·74

1 $3 \cdot 7\square$ and $3 \cdot 7\square$ 2 $2 \cdot 4\square$ and $2 \cdot 4\square$

3 $8 \cdot 1\square$ and $8 \cdot 1\square$ 4 $6 \cdot 0\square$ and $6 \cdot 0\square$

Find two decimal numbers that are between each pair of numbers.

Practice 9a

1 Copy these and complete them.

1 Half of 0·9
2 4·3 multiplied by 7
3 22 + 18 + 36 = ____
4 Double 2·3
5 Half of 720
6 12 times 7
7 1 × 100 = ____
8 990 ÷ 1000 = ____
9 Multiply 0·6 by 8

2 Approximate, then work out the answers to the multiplications.

1 2·67 × 4 = ☐
2 3·09 × 7 = ☐
3 8·54 × 6 = ☐
4 7·15 × 9 = ☐
5 0·98 × 8 = ☐
6 5·63 × 7 = ☐

3 Choose two equivalent fractions from the box.

$\frac{1}{2} = \frac{2}{4}$

$\frac{1}{2}$	$\frac{2}{3}$	$\frac{15}{20}$	$\frac{5}{15}$	$\frac{10}{30}$
$\frac{4}{6}$	$\frac{3}{4}$	$\frac{70}{100}$	$\frac{2}{4}$	$\frac{7}{10}$

Find five different pairs of equivalent fractions.

4 Write three decimal numbers that are between each pair of numbers.

6·72 and 6·73
→ 6·726

1 6·72 and 6·73
2 4·95 and 4·96
3 7·08 and 7·09
4 3·2 and 3·21
5 1·99 and 2
6 5 and 5·01

5 Copy and complete the four products with different pairs of numbers.

☐ × ☐ = 24   ☐ × ☐ = 24

☐ × ☐ = 24   ☐ × ☐ = 24

Do the same for answers 30, 54 and 72.

Practice 9b

1 Copy these and write the missing numbers.

1. ☐ × 10 = 2890
2. 688 + ☐ = 1402
3. 60 + 20 + ☐ = 120
4. ☐ times 9 = 108
5. ☐ divided into 78 = 13
6. Double ☐ = 0·44
7. Half of ☐ = 470
8. ☐ × 7 = 49
9. 54 ÷ ☐ = 6

2 Write these decimal measurements in figures.

1. Five metres and fifty-five hundredths of a metre.
2. Eighty-eight kilometres and eight tenths of a kilometre.
3. Three hundred thousandths of a litre.
4. Two kilograms and two hundredths of a kilogram.

3 Calculate each proportion as a percentage, using a calculator if necessary, and round to the nearest whole percentage.

1. 2 out of 3
2. 5 out of 7
3. 3 out of 8
4. 4 out of 9
5. 7 out of 11
6. 5 out of 8

4 Write the ratio of the number of triangles in the two shapes.

1. 2 to 4 → 1 to 2

Write each ratio in its simplest form.

1
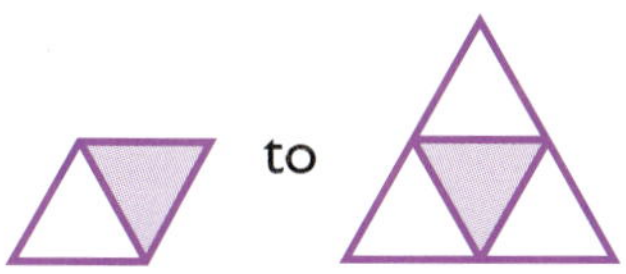

2
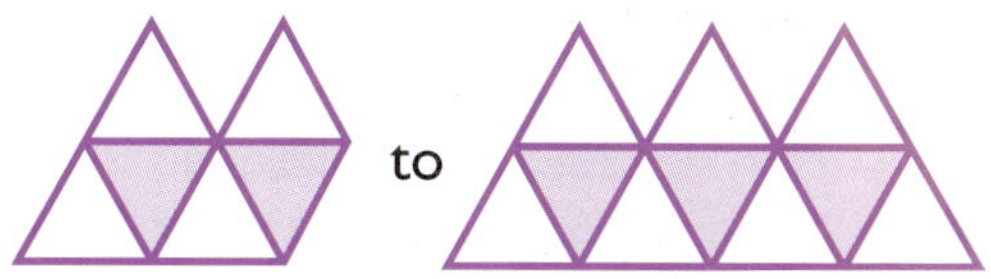

3

4

5 Copy the decimal multiplication.
Choose four digits from the oval to complete the calculation.
Work out the answer.

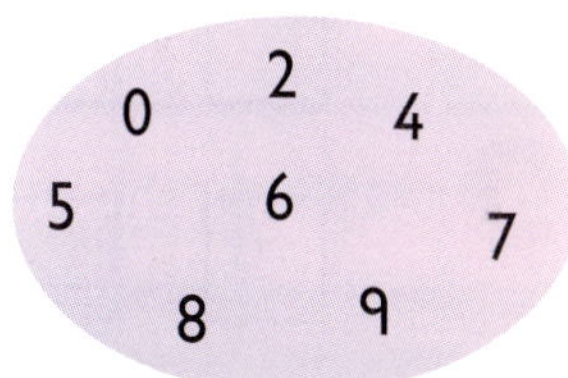

☐•☐☐ × ☐ = ☐

Check the answer by approximating. Repeat with four more sets of digits.

Practice 10a

1 Copy these and complete them.

1	80 + 40 + 20 = ____	2	Half of 6·6	3	47 × 25 = ____
4	Divide 8 by 10	5	Double 37	6	19 ÷ 6 = ____
7	11 multiplied by 11	8	3·9 × 10 = ____	9	66 times 6

2 Cancel each fraction and write it in its simplest form.

$\frac{5}{10} = \frac{1}{2}$

$\frac{5}{10}$ $\frac{4}{6}$ $\frac{24}{32}$ $\frac{90}{100}$ $\frac{33}{55}$ $\frac{40}{64}$ $\frac{27}{54}$ $\frac{35}{42}$

3

1 Gavin has 10 conkers. He gives 1 in every 5 of his conkers to Isabel. How many conkers does he keep for himself?

2 In a box of 45 chocolates, 2 in every 3 are milk chocolates. How many are milk chocolates?

3 At a tennis course 3 in every 4 children are girls. There are 24 children on the course. How many boys and how many girls are on the tennis course?

4 At a bowling party there are 15 children, 3 of whom are boys. What proportion of the children are boys and what proportion are girls?

4 Write the proportion of shaded squares in each shape.

1 in 3 is shaded

1 

2 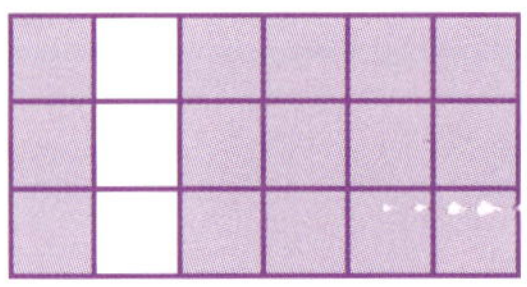

3 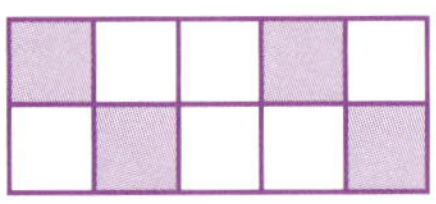

4 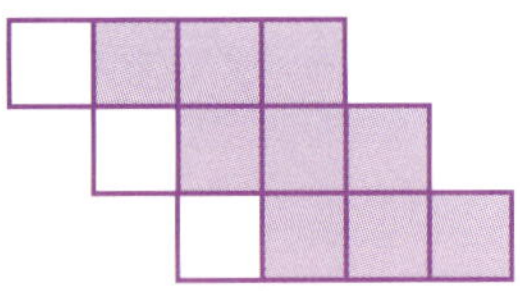

5 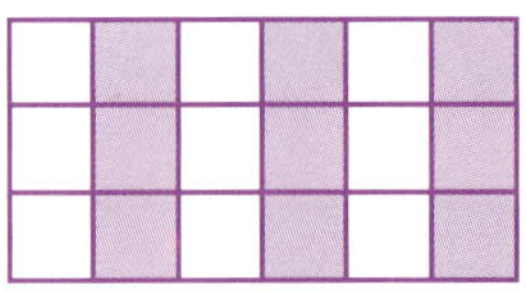

6 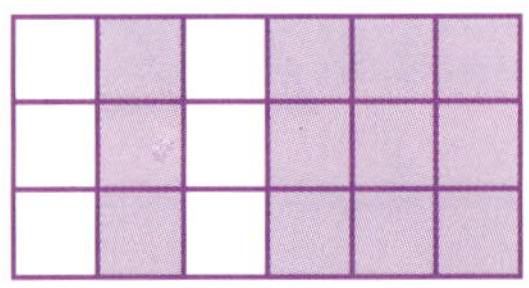

5 Copy these and write what the missing numbers could be. You may use a calculator.

1 [ ]•[ ][ ] × [ ] = 21·84

2 [ ]•[ ][ ] × [ ] = 7·42

3 [ ]•[ ][ ] × [ ] = 31·14

4 [ ]•[ ][ ] × [ ] = 25·92

Practice 10b

1 Copy these and write the missing numbers.

1	☐ × 10 = 72	2	$\frac{3}{4} = \frac{9}{\square}$	3	☐ + 90 + 10 = 190
4	☐ times 12 = 144	5	800 ÷ ☐ = 80	6	Divide 133 by ☐ = 19
7	Double ☐ = 2·6	8	Half of ☐ = 840	9	☐ ÷ 7 = 8

2

1 Of the 32 687 spectators at a rugby match, 25 415 were adults. How many were children? You may use a calculator.

2 In a theatre each of the 32 rows has 53 seats. How many seats are there in the theatre? You may use a calculator.

3 Shaun has 888 stamps in his album shared equally among 37 pages. How many stamps are on each page? You may use a calculator.

3 Copy the boxes. Match each percentage to its equivalent fraction and decimal.

30%	25%	1%	10%	8%	75%	15%	80%
$\frac{1}{4}$	$\frac{1}{10}$	$\frac{2}{25}$	$\frac{3}{20}$	$\frac{3}{10}$	$\frac{4}{5}$	$\frac{1}{100}$	$\frac{3}{4}$
0·08	0·1	0·3	0·25	0·01	0·75	0·8	0·15

4 Copy the statements. Write in the words 'equally likely' or 'not equally likely' to complete the statements. Explain why the statements are true.

1 When I throw a dice it is ____________ to land on an even or an odd number.

2 It is ____________ that when I break a shoelace it will be the left or the right.

3 It is ____________ that the next person to enter the classroom will be an adult or a child.

4 Buttered toast is ____________ to land butter-side down or butter-side up.

5 Make up a difficult calculation which uses brackets and two of the operations +, –, × or ÷.

(27 x 31) + 936 = 1773

Work out the answer with a calculator. Repeat for five different calculations.

Practice 11a

1 Copy these and complete them.

1. $3927 \times 6 =$ ____
2. Double 80 = ____
3. Two eighteens
4. $192 \times 1000 =$ ____
5. Multiply 9 by 0·6
6. What is 80^2?
7. Double 4·9
8. $7{\cdot}2 \div 8 =$ ____
9. $7 \times 0{\cdot}4 =$ ____

2 Copy these statements. Write whether they are true or false. Explain why.

1. A coin is equally likely to land heads as it is to land tails.
2. A rolled dice is equally likely to land showing a number less than 3 as it is a number greater than or equal to 3.
3. When I am asked to write my name it is equally likely that I will use my right hand as it is I will use my left hand.

3 You may use a calculator to solve these.

1. The area of a rectangle is 2744 cm^2. The length and breadth are whole numbers of centimetres. How many centimetres long is each?
2. 986 adults pay £15 and 587 children pay £12 to go to a concert. What is the total amount paid?
3. Find two consecutive odd numbers with a product of 3363.

4 Throw a 1–6 dice 20 times and record the scores.

What is the mode of the scores?

Do this again four more times.

Is the mode the same every time? Explain your answer.

score	frequency
1	
2	
3	
4	
5	
6	

5 Copy this diagram three times.

Write a different percentage in the top box of each diagram. Write in their boxes the fractions and decimals equivalent to the percentages.
Do this again, starting with fractions, and then again, starting with decimals.

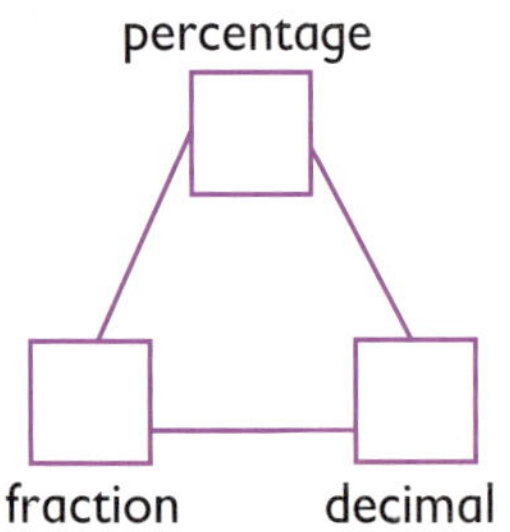

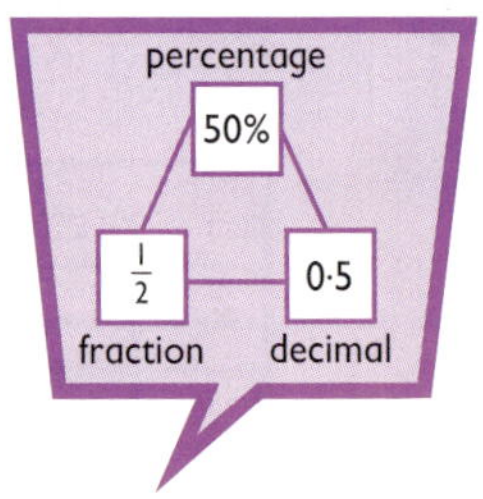

Practice 11b

1 Copy these and write the missing numbers.

1 ☐ + 36 = 100
2 5 × ☐ = 500
3 32 + ☐ + 27 = 77
4 ☐ ÷ 10 = 9·5
5 ☐ × 2 = 7800
6 6 by divided ☐ = **0·6**
7 1940 ÷ ☐ = 970
8 ☐ × 6 = 36
9 $\frac{1}{4}$ of £200

2

1 1% of £354 = ☐
2 20% of 945 kg = ☐
3 70% of 283 l = ☐
4 40% of 730 m = ☐
5 75% of £21.52 = ☐
6 33% of £4.20 = ☐

3

1 On a hotel breakfast table the ratio of packets of rice crispies to cornflakes is 2 to 3. Altogether there are 20 packets. How many are cornflakes?

2 In a primary school there are 350 children. The ratio of boys to girls is 3 to **4.** How many boys and how many girls are there in the school?

3 In each hour from 9 a.m. to 12 midday the ratio of single-decker to double-decker buses passing a school is 2 to 5. In any hour 14 buses pass the school. How many single-decker buses pass the school in the three hours?

4 On a 1–6 dice, what is the probability of:

1 rolling a 6
2 rolling an odd number
3 rolling a number less than 3
4 rolling a 0
5 rolling a number from 1 to 6?

Show each of the probabilities on a 0 to 1 probability scale.

5 Copy the table. Roll a 1–12 dice 5 times and record the results. Write in the range after 5 rolls.

number of times rolled	5	10	15	20	25	30	35	40	**45**	**50**
range of scores										

Do this again, finding the **total** range each time.

Explain why the range of the scores is not always 11.

Practice 12a

1 Copy these and complete them.

1 28 + 72 = ____ **2** 18 × 24 = ____ **3** 38 ÷ 10 = ____

4 0·04 × 10 = ____ **5** 715 + 679 = ____ **6** Divide 4·5 by 9

7 Half of 76 **8** Multiply 35 × 4 **9** 0·6 × 30 = ____

2 Haroun says, 'If I toss a coin it is equally likely to be a head as a tail'.

The table shows what happens after Haroun tosses a coin 20 times.

H	T
13	7

Explain why the results are not 10 heads and 10 tails.

3

1 How many children took the test?

2 How many questions do you think there were in the test?

3 Why do you think the highest frequency occurred in the 21–30 range?

4 How many children do you think got more than half of the questions correct?

Number of children getting ranges of marks in a maths test

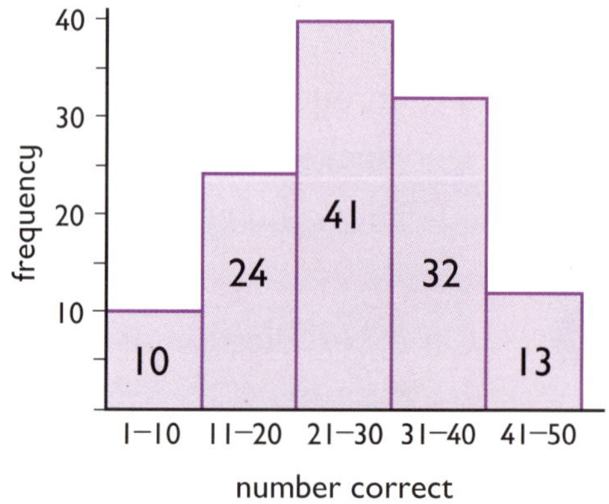

4 Copy the statements. Write if a statement is always true, sometimes true or always false. Explain why.

1 A rectangle has four right angles.

2 A square is a parallelogram.

3 A trapezium has both pairs of opposite sides parallel.

4 The diagonals of a rhombus are equal.

5 Draw these quadrilaterals.

1 a square **2** a rectangle **3** a parallelogram **4** a rhombus

Draw all the axes of symmetry in each shape.

Practice 12b

1 Copy these and write the missing numbers.

1	49 + ☐ = 100	2	28 + 82 + ☐ = 1323	3	$\frac{\square}{5} = \frac{8}{10}$
4	2 ÷ ☐ = 0·2	5	☐ multiplied by 6 = 126	6	Double ☐ = 7·4
7	0·7 × ☐ = 7	8	☐ ÷ 2 = 260	9	☐ ÷ 9 = 7

2

1. The proportion of boys in a class is 2 in every 5 children. What percentage of the class are boys? What percentage are girls?
2. In a packet of pastilles 1 in every 4 is black. What percentage of the pastilles are black? What percentage are not black?
3. In a crate of bananas 1 in every 50 is bad. What percentage of the bananas are good?

3

1. How many matches did Ramchester United play in the season?
2. What was the highest score in any match? Explain how you decided.
3. Russell says, 'Ramchester scored 1 goal in as many matches as they scored 3 goals'. Is he right/maybe right/not right? Explain how you decided.

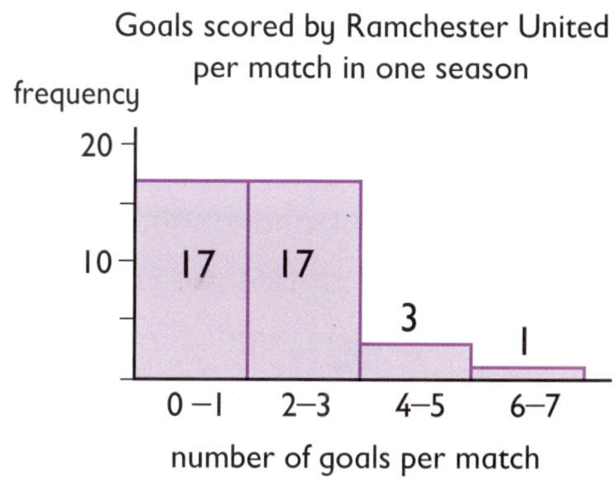

4 Draw these shapes:

1. a quadrilateral which has 0 lines of symmetry
2. a quadrilateral which has exactly 1 line of symmetry
3. a quadrilateral which has exactly 2 lines of symmetry
4. a quadrilateral which has exactly 4 lines of symmetry.

5 Copy the multiplication. Use the digits 1 to 5 in any order to complete the multiplication. Work out the answer.

☐☐☐☐ × ☐ = ☐

Find the order of the digits 1 to 5 which gives the largest possible answer.
Find the order of the digits 1 to 5 which gives the smallest possible answer.

Practice 13a

1 Copy these and complete them.

1	133 divided by 7	2	Double 0·14	3	8·8 × 1000 = ____
4	67 + 33 = ____	5	40 ÷ 100 = ____	6	Half of 1560
7	Double 270	8	Divide 36 by 8	9	What is 50^2?

2

1 Find the mean of a pair of numbers in the circle.
Do this three times.

2 Find the mean of a trio of numbers in the circle.
Do this three times.

3 Find the mean of the four numbers in the circle.

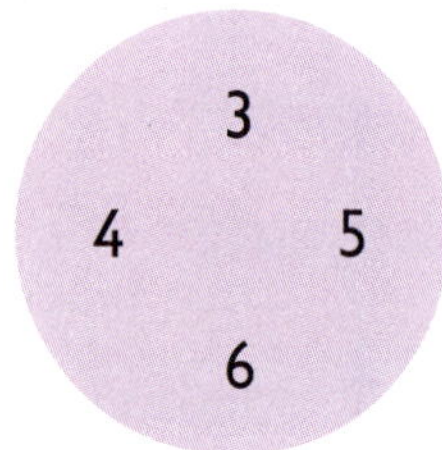

3

1 What are the coordinates of the four vertices of the square ABCD?

2 The square is translated 2 squares right and 1 square down.
What are the coordinates of the vertices of the square in its new position?

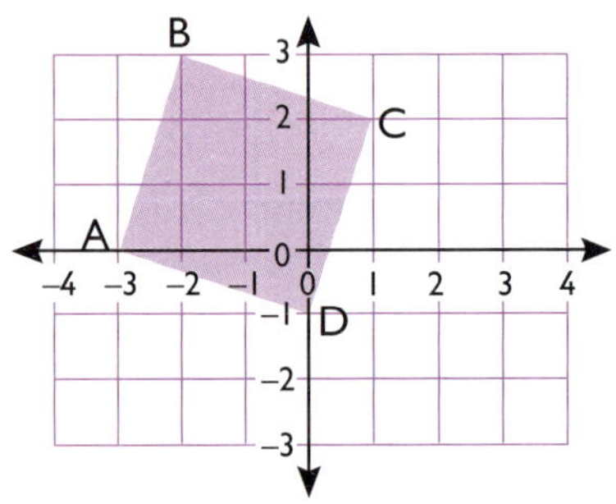

4 Copy the calculations and find the answers. Write about how you did them.

1	33 × 34	2	666 ÷ 44	3	12·5% of £35 000

5 On squared paper make two copies of this 2-square shape.

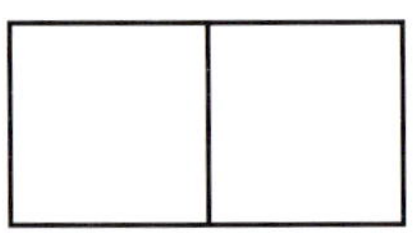

Draw the two shapes together to make a new shape so that the squares fit exactly side-to-side.
Do this as many times as you can.
Which of your 4-square shapes have reflective symmetry?
Can you add one square to any of the shapes to make the net of an open cube?
Are there some shapes you *can't* do this for?

Practice 13b

1 Copy these and write the missing numbers.

1	1528 × ▢ = 9168	2	▢ + 250 = 1000	3	▢ × 100 = 1600
4	▢ ÷ 10 = 0·06	5	▢ + 65 + 35 = 163	6	▢ multiplied by 41 = 0
7	38 ÷ ▢ = 0·38	8	166 × ▢ = 332	9	Half of ▢ = 33

2 Test 1 was on a Monday. Test 2 was on the Friday, after some revision.

1 Who scored the highest mark in each test?

2 Who scored a total of 13 out of 20?

3 Whose score increased by 50% from Test 1 to Test 2?

Marks out of 10 in two mental maths tests					
	Aisha	Gary	Nigel	Jake	Masie
Test 1	4	6	3	5	7
Test 2	6	8	3	8	9

3 Copy and complete the statements.

1	10 cm = ▢ mm	2	10 m = ▢ km	3	10 m = ▢ cm
4	10 km = ▢ m	5	10 mm = ▢ cm	6	10 cm = ▢ m
7	10 km = ▢ mm	8	10 mm = ▢ km	9	10 km = ▢ cm

4 Calculate the perimeters of the shapes. All the units are centimetres.

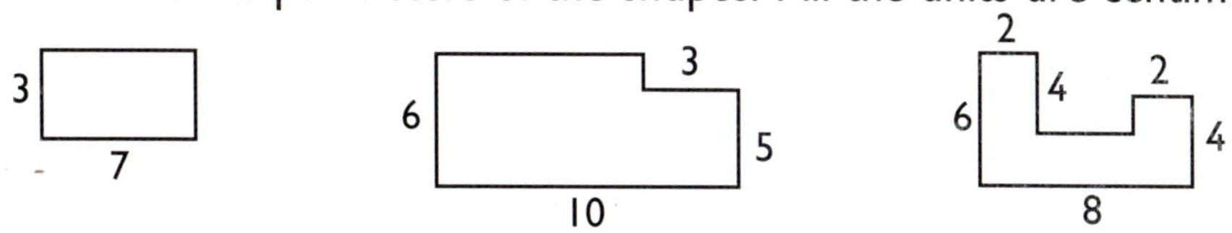

5 Draw a parallelogram and write a mathematical property that is common to all parallelograms.

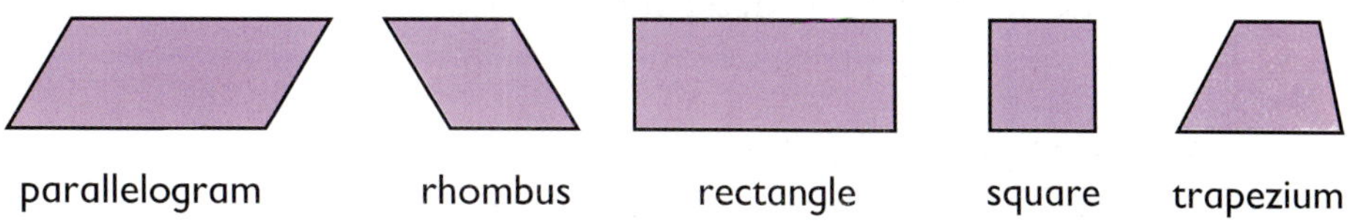

Do the same for the other shapes.

Practice 14a

1 Copy these and complete them.

1	16 × 32 = _____	2	1750 ÷ 2 = _____	3	450 + 550 = _____
4	55 × 1000 = _____	5	Multiply 0·8 by 0·5	6	0·4 times 7
7	0·08 × 100 = _____	8	50 + 60 + 40 = _____	9	Double 660

2 Draw a coordinate grid on squared paper.

Draw a triangle on the grid.

What are the coordinates of its vertices?

Draw the triangle when it has been translated 2 squares up and 1 square to the left.

Do this again for a quadrilateral and then for a pentagon.

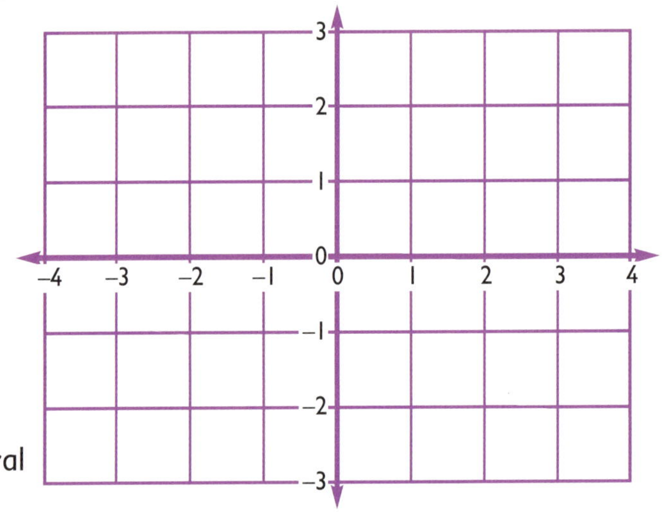

3 Measure the perimeter of a rectangular book.

Repeat for five more books.

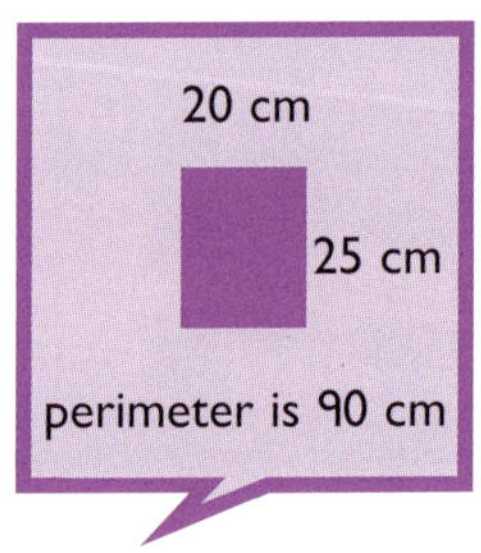

4 Copy the statements. Write in the correct numbers in the boxes.

1	500 g = ☐ kg	2	750 ml = ☐ l	3	250 mm = ☐ cm
4	850 cm = ☐ m	5	1300 g = ☐ kg	6	4800 ml = ☐ l
7	50 mm = ☐ m	8	100 cm = ☐ km	9	10 ml = ☐ l

5 Write what you know about Greenwich Mean Time (GMT) and British Summer Time (BST).

Give some examples to illustrate the relationship between GMT and BST.

Practice 14b

1 Copy these and write the missing numbers.

1	350 + □ = 1000	2	2700 ÷ □ = 27	3	222 × □ = 22 200
4	40 + □ + 44 = 126	5	2·73 times □ = 27·3	6	Half of □ = 0·35
7	Double □ = 0·96	8	16 × □ = 512	9	9 × □ = 72

2 From the box choose:

3	3	4	4	5	5	6	6	7	7

1. three numbers with a median of 6
2. four numbers with a median of 6
3. five numbers with a median of 5
4. six numbers with a median of 5

3 Copy and complete the sentences.

1. I would measure the length of ______________________ in metres.
2. I would measure the length of ______________________ in millimetres.
3. I would measure the length of ______________________ in kilometres.
4. I would measure the length of ______________________ in centimetres.

4 On squared paper copy the coordinate grid.

Plot the points that are corners of a quadrilateral. Write the coordinates of each corner.

Do this again for an isosceles triangle, a pentagon and a hexagon.

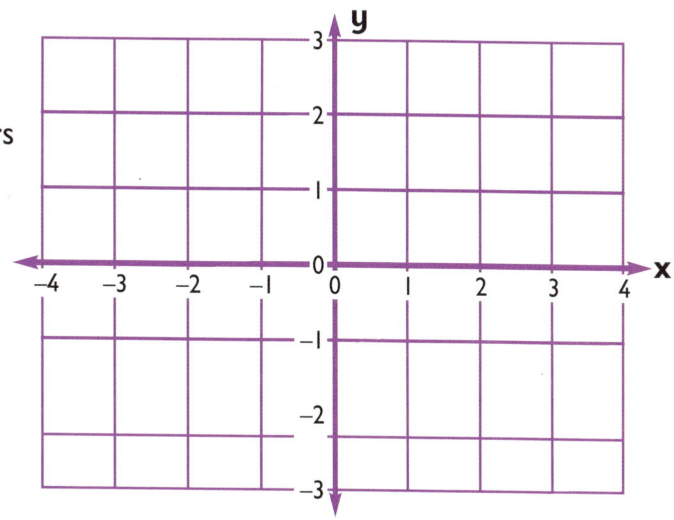

5 Draw a rectangle.

Investigate the different shapes that can be made using one straight cut.

Do this again for two straight cuts.

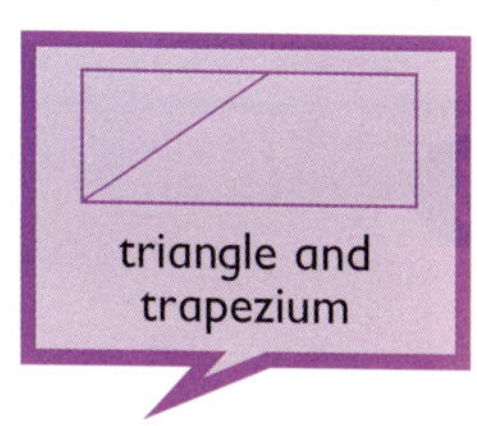

Practice 15a

1 Copy these and complete them.

1	Add 3690 to 4183	2	150 + 850 = ____	3	0·01 × 1000 = ____
4	7359 + 1864 = ____	5	6300 + 1800 = ____	6	340 take away 190
7	4963 − 2741 = ____	8	6000 ÷ 1000 = ____	9	438 × 42 = ____

2 Use centimetre-squared paper to draw an L-shape which has a perimeter of 20 cm.

Do this in four different ways.

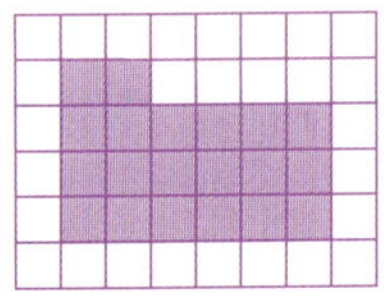

3

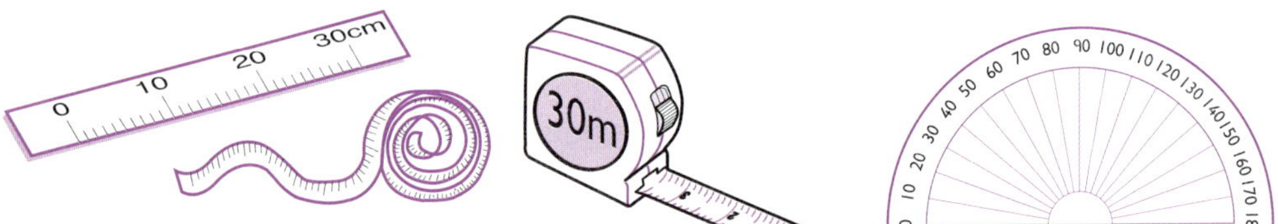

Which instrument would you use to measure:

1 the length of a nail?

2 the perimeter of a classroom?

3 the diameter of a large tractor wheel?

4 the perimeter of a bicycle wheel?

4 Copy and complete the time chart of cities around the world.

New York	London	Berlin	Hong Kong	Tokyo	Sydney
07:00	12:00	13:00	20:00	21:00	22:00
	18:00				
	midnight				

5 Copy the incomplete calculations. Each symbol is the same number in each calculation.

Find what they are.

□ × △ = 7680 □ ÷ △ = 7·5

□ + △ = 272 □ − △ = 208

Write about how you found them.

Practice 15b

1 Copy these and write the missing numbers.

1	$\square + 0{\cdot}4 = 1$	2	$\square + 1700 = 3500$	3	$\frac{1}{\square} = \frac{4}{12}$
4	$51 + 53 + \square = 159$	5	$\square$ times $100 = 210$	6	$\square + 26 = 52$
7	$\square \times 10 = 2{\cdot}6$	8	Half of $\square = 4{\cdot}2$	9	$\square \div 100 = 8{\cdot}3$

2 Copy and complete the grid.

size of rectangle	8 cm by 5 cm	10 m by 19 m	25 km by 16 km	28 cm by 0·5 m
perimeter				

3 Draw the shape on squared paper.

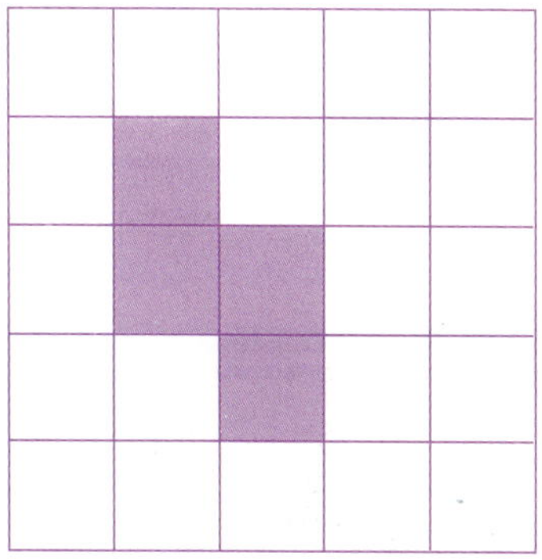

Translate the shape according to the instructions:

3 left, 4 up, 2 right, 1 up.

Draw the shape in its new position.

Repeat for these instructions, starting from the same place each time:

1 2 right, 3 down, 1 right, 2 up.

2 1 down, 1 up, 3 right, 4 down.

4 Measure and record:

1 the height of your classroom

2 the thickness of this book

3 the thickness of your little finger

4 the length and the width of a table.

5 Copy the incomplete addition.

$\square\,\square\,0\,0 + \square\,\square\,0\,0 = 6\,3\,0\,0$

Find as many different ways as you can of correctly completing the addition.

Practice 16a

1 Copy these and complete them.

1	$0{\cdot}1 \times 0{\cdot}9 =$ ____	2	Double 0·26	3	$5647 + 3658 =$ ____
4	$80 - 40 =$ ____	5	Sum of 271 and 429	6	$425 \times 10 =$ ____
7	Square 40	8	$4400 + 2700 =$ ____	9	41 multiplied by 0

2 Copy the table and the grid.

Cooking times	
chicken	20 mins per pound plus 20 mins
lamb	30 mins per pound plus 30 mins

Complete the grid.

Number of pounds	3	4·5	6	7·5	10
Cooking time for chicken					
Cooking time for lamb					

3 Copy the two incomplete numbers. Choose any digits to complete them.

Find the sum and difference of the two numbers.

		0	0

		0	0

Do this for six pairs of numbers.

4 Copy the additions and subtractions. If you can, find the answers mentally. If not, use jottings. If you still can't do them, use a calculator.

1	$3000 + 7000$	2	$4988 - 1736$	3	$2226 + 6662$
4	$2603 + 1201$	5	$8072 - 1659$	6	$9500 - 6700$

For each calculation write whether you did it mentally, with jottings or used a calculator.

5 Choose two sequence rules from the box.

Write the first ten numbers in each sequence, starting from 0.

Write two numbers which will appear in both sequences. (You may need to extend the sequences.)

Do this for four pairs of sequences.

count on in 6s
count on in 7s
count on in 8s
count on in 9s

Practice 16b

1 Copy these and write the missing numbers.

1	$13^2 =$ □	2	□ $+ 0{\cdot}3 = 0{\cdot}38$	3	□ $+ 3418 = 7809$
4	$70 \div$ □ $= 0{\cdot}7$	5	Double □ $= 1{\cdot}4$	6	$54 +$ □ $= 108$
7	□ $\times 1000 = 8000$	8	Half of □ $= 0{\cdot}32$	9	□ $\times 24 = 408$

2 Copy the sequences and find the numbers hidden behind the clouds.

1 ☁ $\xrightarrow{-8}$ ☁ $\xrightarrow{-8}$ ☁ $\xrightarrow{-8}$ 15 $\xrightarrow{-8}$ ☁ $\xrightarrow{-8}$ ☁ $\xrightarrow{-8}$ ☁

2 ☁ $\xrightarrow{-25}$ ☁ $\xrightarrow{-25}$ 66 $\xrightarrow{-25}$ ☁ $\xrightarrow{-25}$ ☁ $\xrightarrow{-25}$ ☁ $\xrightarrow{-25}$ ☁

3 ☁ $\xrightarrow{-13}$ ☁ $\xrightarrow{-13}$ ☁ $\xrightarrow{-13}$ ☁ $\xrightarrow{-13}$ 23 $\xrightarrow{-13}$ ☁ $\xrightarrow{-13}$ ☁

3 Choose a number from each box and find their product.

3·84	2·09	1·67

6	7	8	9

$1{\cdot}67 \times 6 = 10{\cdot}02$

Do this for six pairs.

4 Copy the table of cities and times.

Copy the sorting grid. Sort the cities according to whether their time zone is east of London, the same as London or to the west of London.

Time zones		
east of London	same as London	west of London

Standard time at 12:00 GMT	
Athens	14:00
Bombay	17:30
Chicago	06:00
Darwin	21:30
Dublin	12:00
Québec	07:00
Glasgow	12:00

5 Copy the incomplete subtraction. Choose eight digits from the box to complete it.

□	□	□	□	−	□	□	□	□	=	1	5	2	9

Do the same for the answers 4083, 6175 and 7889.

0 1 2 3 4 5 6 7 8 9

Practice 17a

1 Copy these and complete them.

1	Take 600 from 1378	2	30 + 30 = ____	3	What is 11^2?
4	0·27 × 100 = ____	5	370 ÷ 2 = ____	6	6102 – 4931 = ____
7	47 + 46 + 13 = ____	8	Half of 0·42	9	14·7 ÷ 7 = ____

2

1. In three football matches Colford Town had attendances of 52 947, 58 496 and 57 824.
   What was the total attendance for the three matches?
2. At a two day pop festival, 79 286 people came on the first day. This was increased by 3642 on the second day. How many people went on the second day?
3. In October 17 832 people used Knock Airport. The following month 1792 more used the airport. How many people used the airport in November?

3 Find all the numbers less than 50 that can be written as the difference of two square numbers.

$5^2 - 2^2 = 21$

4

1. How far is it from Edinburgh to London?
2. Shaun travels from Cardiff to Plymouth via Manchester.
   What is the total distance he travels?
3. Approximately, how many kilometres is it from Cardiff to Manchester?

8 kilometres ≈ 5 miles

	Cardiff	Edinburgh	Leeds	Manchester	London
Edinburgh	385				
Leeds	219	202			
Manchester	172	215	40		
London	159	378	189	185	
Plymouth	163	496	316	283	210

Distances are in miles

5 Copy the two incomplete decimal numbers. Choose digits from the box to complete the two numbers. Find their difference.

Do this for six pairs of numbers. $\square.\square - \square.\square\square$

Digits: 4 1 5 2 3

Which set of five digits gives the largest difference?

Which set of five digits gives the smallest difference?

Practice 17b

1 Copy these and write the missing numbers.

1	☐ + 77 = 154	2	3400 + ☐ = 7300	3	0·05 + ☐ = 0·75
4	☐ − 1413 = 2211	5	☐ times 2 = 1·5	6	Half of ☐ = 0·41
7	☐ ÷ 100 = 0·01	8	Double ☐ = 38	9	Half of ☐ = 2·9

2 Choose a number from each box. Find their sum and difference.

436	1905	28 370

927	3418	56 079

Do this five times.

3 Copy and complete the table.

Attendances at four football clubs in a season			
club	greatest	least	range
Colford Rovers	37 093	21 846	
Chelwater Rovers	50 047	47 915	
Halford City	16 208	14 713	
Access United	29 430	11 059	

4 Copy the triangular number sequence and write the number of squares in the empty boxes.

Draw the next three shapes in the sequence with their numbers.

What is the value of the triangular number which has 10 squares along its bottom row?

5 Copy the blank addition. Each of the three numbers uses the four digits 0, 1, 3 and 5. Complete the addition.

☐☐☐☐ + ☐☐☐☐ = ☐☐☐☐

Practice 18a

1 Copy these and complete them.

1	Double 1400	2	2·37 multiplied by 10	3	900 + 900 = ____
4	0·7 × 1000 = ____	5	27 × 18 = ____	6	7084 − 2966 = ____
7	180 − 90 = ____	8	(357 ÷ 17) + 79 = ____	9	Total 4500 and 7500

2 Copy the three blank boxes. Use all the digits 1 to 9 to complete the numbers.

Find the sum and difference of one pair of numbers.

Do this for three different pairs.

$$\begin{array}{r} 496 \\ +\,173 \\ \hline \end{array} \qquad \begin{array}{r} 496 \\ -\,173 \\ \hline \end{array}$$

3 Write the numbers in each box in order, smallest first.

19	−21	7	−11

0	9	−47	74

−32	23	32	−23

86	−68	68	−86

4 Copy and extend the sequences.

1 1 4 9 16 ____ ____ ____ ____

2 1 3 6 10 ____ ____ ____ ____

3 1 3 7 15 ____ ____ ____ ____

5 Copy the incomplete addition. Use eight of the digits 0 to 9 to complete the two numbers so that the sum is 6000.

$$\begin{array}{r} \square\square\square\square \\ +\,\square\square\square\square \\ \hline 6\,0\,0\,0 \end{array}$$

Find different ways of doing this.

Do this again for the sums 7000, 8000 and 9000.

Practice 18b

1 Copy these and write the missing numbers.

1	□ + 2800 = 6200	2	19 × □ = 969	3	(41 − 17) + □ = 760
4	11 × □ = 11 000	5	□ + 2694 = 8222	6	19^2 = □
7	7512 − □ = 5669	8	5000 ÷ □ = 5	9	0·4 times □ = 2·8

2 Copy the two incomplete decimal numbers. Choose three digits from the oval to complete the numbers.

Find the sum and difference of the two decimal numbers.

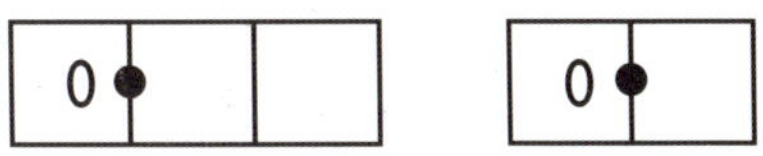

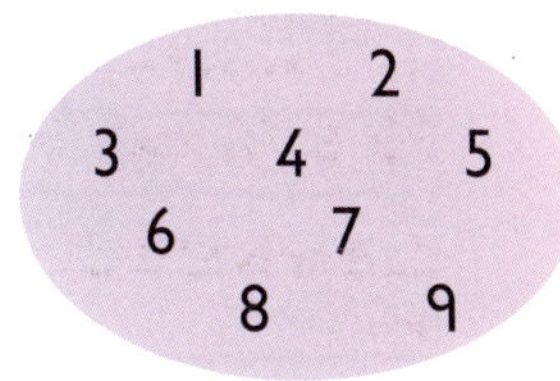

Do this for four pairs of numbers.

3 The 08:30 train from London to Edinburgh left King's Cross 35 minutes late. It made up 8 minutes of lost time on its journey. It was due to arrive at Edinburgh at 13:08.

1 At what time did the train arrive in Edinburgh?

2 A plane from London to Edinburgh takes 1 hour 15 minutes. By how much is the plane faster than the train, when the train runs on time?

4 Copy and extend the triangular number sequence. Write in each empty box the sum of the two numbers above it.

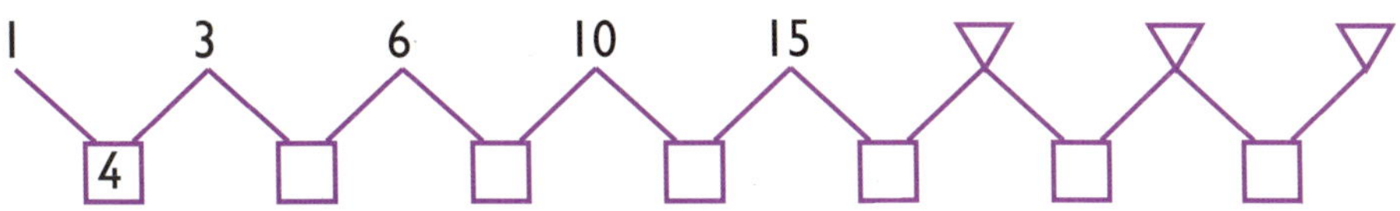

What do you notice?

5 Use a calculator and these instructions to generate a number sequence. Write each number in the sequence.

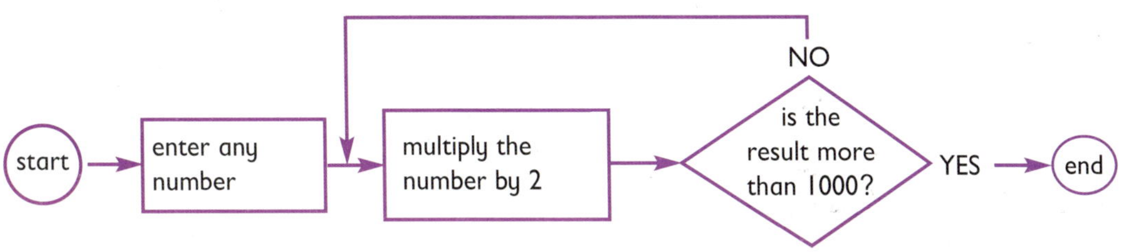

Do this three times.

Practice 19a

1 Copy these and complete them.

1 5800 + 6500 = _____
2 1200 – 600 = _____
3 Subtract 230 from 649
4 17 × 51 = _____
5 53 + 53 = _____
6 6800 + 6800 = _____
7 9 ÷ 10 = _____
8 What is 15 squared?
9 333 × 100 = _____

2 Copy and complete the foreign exchange table.

Currency	Exchange rate	Number of pounds sterling	Equivalent in foreign currency
European Union	£1 = €1·61	£100	€ ☐
Switzerland	£1 = 2·65 francs	£250	☐ francs
Greece	£1 = 556 drachma	£500	☐ drachma
United States	£1 = $1·46	£350	$ ☐

3 Find approximate answers for the divisions.

1 915 ÷ 32
2 489 ÷ 53
3 794 ÷ 78

Now work out the correct answers.

4 Copy the table.

Complete the range of temperatures for each continent.

Continent	Record highest temperature	Record lowest temperature	Range
Africa	58°C	–24°C	
North America	57°C	–63°C	
South America	49°C	–33°C	
Europe	50°C	–55°C	
Antarctica	15°C	–89°C	
Asia	54°C	–70°C	
Australasia	51°C	–23°C	

5 Copy and complete the multiplications.

31 × 10 = ☐
31 × 3 = ☐
31 × 13 = ☐

Do the same to find the answers to 48 × 12, 57 × 15 and 82 × 14.

Practice 19b

1 Copy these and write the missing numbers.

1	20 + ☐ = 40	**2**	6600 + ☐ = 14 200	**3**	0·09 × ☐ = 0·9
4	☐ − 3·5 = 6·5	**5**	☐ × 4 = 228	**6**	11 times ☐ = 121
7	0·74 + ☐ = 1·24	**8**	☐ ÷ 1000 = 0·44	**9**	20^2 = ☐

2 Write in the coordinates of the corners of each triangle.

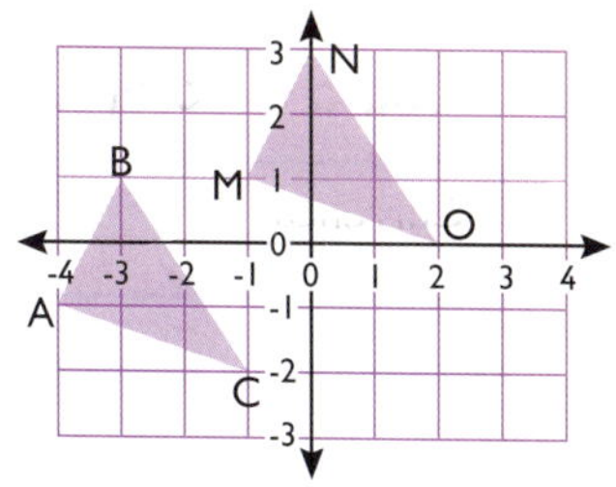

A (☐, ☐) translates to M (☐, ☐)

B (☐, ☐) translates to N (☐, ☐)

C (☐, ☐) translates to O (☐, ☐)

Write instructions that perform this translation.

3 Copy this statement and complete the approximation for 85·8 ÷ 6.

85·8 ÷ 6 —is approximately→ 84 ÷ 6 = ☐

Work out the exact answer of 85·8 ÷ 6 as a mixed number.

Find approximations and accurate answers for these divisions.

80·1 ÷ 9   53·2 ÷ 7   75·2 ÷ 8   129·6 ÷ 6

4 Copy and complete the diagram to find 285 ÷ 15.

Write about how the diagram works.

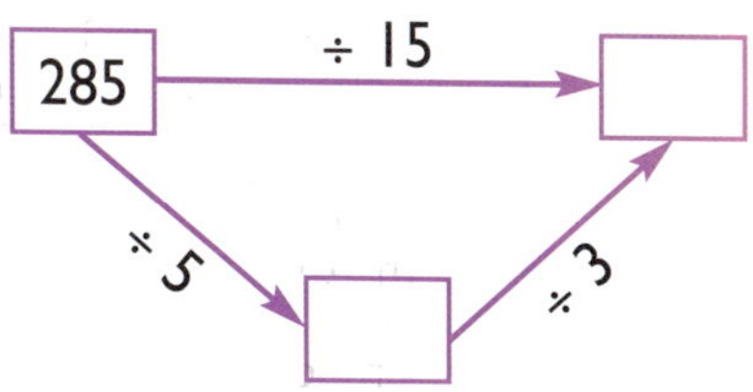

Draw similar diagrams to find the answers to these divisions.

399 ÷ 21   322 ÷ 14   726 ÷ 33

5 Copy the three incomplete multiplications. Choose two numbers from the box and use them in the same order three times to complete the multiplications.

☐☐ × 29 = ____

☐☐ × 30 = ____

☐☐ × 31 = ____

5	6	7
8		9

56 × 29 = ____

56 × 30 = ____

56 × 31 = ____

Write about how you worked out the answers.

Do this four times, with different pairs of digits.

Practice 20a

1 Copy these and complete them.

1	39 + 55 + 25 = ____	**2**	70 + 70 = ____	**3**	827 – 127 = ____
4	1 – 0·3 = ____	**5**	Increase 85 by 115	**6**	8 ÷ 100 = ____
7	108 – 54 = ____	**8**	Half of 9·2	**9**	Double 3900

2 Copy and extend the sequences.

1 18 $\xrightarrow{-7}$ 11 $\xrightarrow{-7}$ 4 $\xrightarrow{-7}$ –3 $\xrightarrow{-7}$ ☐ $\xrightarrow{-7}$ ☐ $\xrightarrow{-7}$ ☐ $\xrightarrow{-7}$ ☐

2 36 $\xrightarrow{-11}$ 25 $\xrightarrow{-11}$ 14 $\xrightarrow{-11}$ 3 $\xrightarrow{-11}$ ☐ $\xrightarrow{-11}$ ☐ $\xrightarrow{-11}$ ☐ $\xrightarrow{-11}$ ☐

3 29 $\xrightarrow{-9}$ 20 $\xrightarrow{-9}$ 11 $\xrightarrow{-9}$ ☐ $\xrightarrow{-9}$ ☐ $\xrightarrow{-9}$ ☐ $\xrightarrow{-9}$ ☐ $\xrightarrow{-9}$ ☐

3 Copy and complete the diagram to find 41 x 18.

Draw similar diagrams to answer the multiplications in the box.

32 × 18	55 × 14
36 × 15	

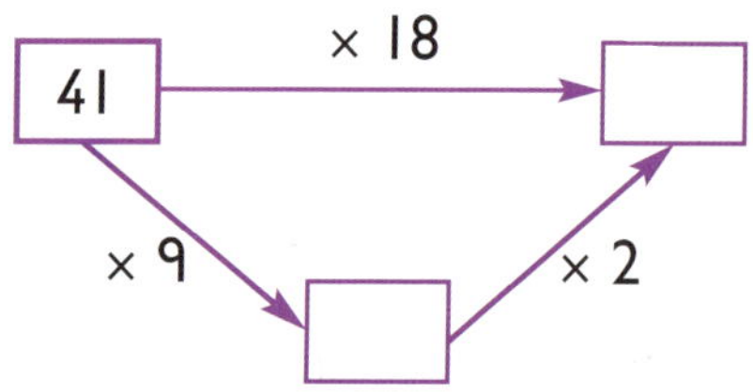

4

1 A £400 freezer has 15% off its price in a sale. What is the price of the freezer in the sale?

2 Four people share the first prize of £78 000 in a Bingo game. How much should each person get?

3 The cost of a holiday is £450 for an adult and £300 for a child. How much would the holiday cost for two adults and three children?

5 Choose three numbers from the box. Use the numbers in the same order to complete the four calculations. Find the answers.

7	9	11	15	20

(□ + △) × ▽ =   □ + (△ × ▽) =

(□ × △) + ▽ =   □ × (△ + ▽) =

Do this for four sets of numbers.

Practice 20b

1 Copy these and write the missing numbers.

1	□ × 49 = 931	2	10 − □ = 6·4	3	□ + 80 = 160
4	5400 − □ = 1600	5	□ − 0·16 = 0·44	6	58 + 13 + □ = 435
7	0·01 × □ = 1	8	30 ÷ □ = 0·03	9	□ − 1876 = 2179

2 Copy the −10 to 10 number line. Write in the empty boxes the numbers the arrows are pointing to. What is the difference between the two numbers?

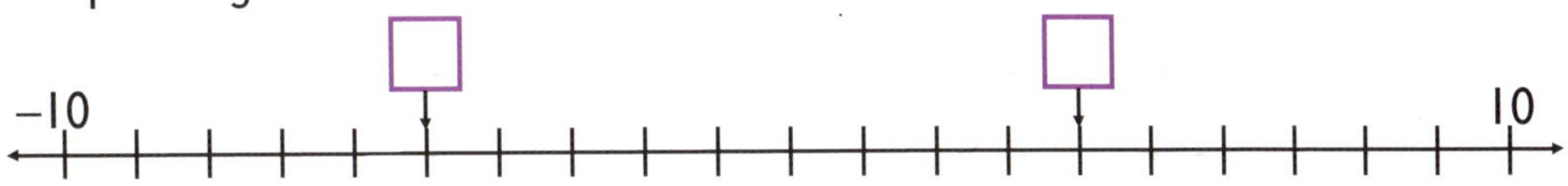

Draw number lines to find the difference between these pairs of numbers.

2 −2	7 −1	3 −8	−6 −9

3

1. What is the ratio of boys to girls in the dance line?
2. There are seven such lines in a dance hall. How many boys and how many girls are dancing altogether?
3. The number of children dancing is increased by 28 in the same ratio. How many girls are there in the dance now?

4 Find two approximations for 972 ÷ 27, then work out the exact answer.

Find two approximations and accurate answers for these divisions.

532 ÷ 14	612 ÷ 34
702 ÷ 26	576 ÷ 64

5 Copy the two blank calculations. Choose three numbers from the oval to complete both calculations correctly.

□ × □ = □   □ ÷ □ = □

3·57   1·4   1·7   1·5   2·1   2·55

Do this three times.

Practice 21a

1 Copy these and complete them.

1	500 subtract 417	2	30 + 32 + 34 = ____	3	Double 5800
4	83 × 10 = ____	5	52 – 26 = ____	6	399 ÷ 21 = ____
7	3250 – 1459 = ____	8	3·2 + 6·8 = ____	9	1102 ÷ 29 = ____

2 Write a number story for each calculation.

Find the answers.

1	3·21 × 15	2	89·46 ÷ 18	3	(25 ÷ 10) × 6

3 Choose a fraction from the first box and a quantity from the second box to make a fraction calculation.

$\frac{2}{3}$	$\frac{3}{4}$	$\frac{4}{5}$

£360	5·4 kg	£48

$\frac{2}{3}$ of £360 = (£360 ÷ 3) × 2
= £120 × 2
= £240

Find the answer. Do this six times.

4 Match a fraction to its equivalent decimal. You may wish to use a calculator to check your matching. Some of the decimals have been rounded to three decimal places.

$\frac{1}{2}$	$\frac{3}{1000}$	$\frac{5}{8}$	$\frac{1}{7}$	$\frac{3}{5}$	$\frac{1}{6}$	$\frac{2}{3}$	$\frac{7}{9}$	$\frac{11}{100}$

0·143	0·5	0·667	0·003	0·778	0·625	0·6	0·11	0·167

Tick each decimal that is an approximate value of its matching fraction.

5 Copy the four incomplete decimal numbers.
Use all the digits in the box to complete the four numbers.

2 0 8 1 5 9 6 4 7 3

Write the four numbers in order, largest first.

0·☐☐ 0·☐☐ 0·☐☐☐ 0·☐☐☐

Do this for five different sets of four decimal numbers.

Practice 21b

1 Copy these and write the missing numbers.

1	300 × ☐ = 600	**2**	☐ − 1600 = 4800	**3**	$\frac{2}{5}$ of ☐ = 80
4	☐ × 1000 = 60	**5**	☐ − 6700 = 6700	**6**	3·4 times ☐ = 23·8
7	3057 + ☐ = 9943	**8**	Double ☐ = 140	**9**	Half of ☐ = 3·7

2 The car costs £15 000 in Britain.

How much cheaper would the car be in pounds if it was bought in Canada, Denmark, Spain or South Africa?

Canada 30 380 dollars

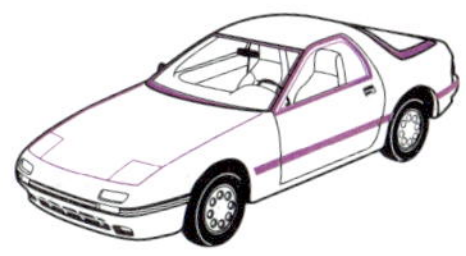

Country	£1 =
Canada	2·17 dollars
Denmark	12·5 kroner
Spain	1·67 euros
South Africa	10·5 rand

Spain 21 209 euros

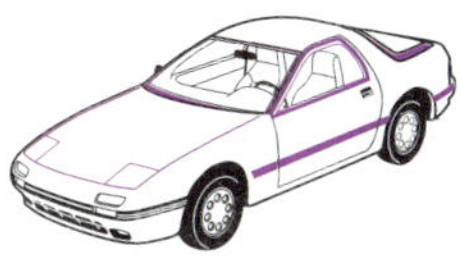

South Africa 118 650 rand

Denmark 168 750 kroner

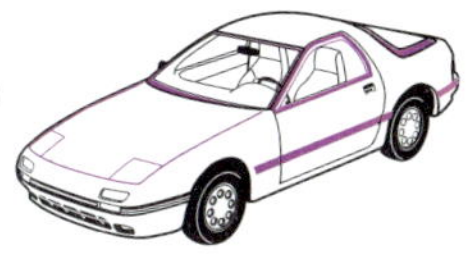

3 Choose two numbers from the box to make a proper fraction.

Use a calculator to change the fraction to a decimal.

Do this for six pairs of numbers.

$\frac{2}{3}$ = 0·67

2	3	4	5	7	10	25	100	1000

4 Copy the blank statement. Choose a fraction from the first circle and a quantity from the second circle to complete the statement. Work out the answer.

$\frac{☐}{☐}$ of ☐ = ______

Do this for five pairs of a fraction and a quantity.

First circle: $\frac{3}{10}$ $\frac{57}{100}$ $\frac{71}{100}$

Second circle: £37 180 kg 150 cm^2 £71 £290

$\frac{3}{10}$ of £290 = £87

5 Copy the two inequalities. Choose digits from the box to complete each inequality correctly. A digit may be used more than once.

$\frac{☐}{☐} < \frac{☐}{☐}$ $\frac{☐}{☐} > \frac{☐}{☐}$

Do this four times.

1	2	3	4	5
6	7	8	9	

Practice 22a

1 Copy these and complete them.

1	Add 470 to 180	**2**	$100 - 54 =$ ____	**3**	$17 \times 49 =$ ____
4	$4600 - 2900 =$ ____	**5**	$(506 \div 23) - 12 =$ ____	**6**	$0{\cdot}5 \times 100 =$ ____
7	$2009 + 7981 =$ ____	**8**	$86{\cdot}1 \div 7 =$ ____	**9**	Multiply 6·3 by 100

2 Write the fractions in each box in order, smallest first. (Changing to equivalent fractions with a common denominator may help.)

$\frac{1}{3}$	$\frac{1}{2}$	$\frac{2}{3}$	$\frac{1}{4}$

$\frac{1}{5}$	$\frac{3}{4}$	$\frac{7}{10}$	$\frac{9}{20}$

$\frac{37}{100}$	$\frac{3}{10}$	$\frac{13}{20}$	$\frac{11}{25}$

3

1	$\frac{1}{10}$ of £400	**2**	$\frac{27}{100}$ of 1 kg	**3**	$\frac{3}{10}$ of 5 m
4	$\frac{9}{100}$ of 3 km	**5**	$\frac{7}{10}$ of 2 litres	**6**	$\frac{59}{100}$ of £6

4 Draw each shape accurately using a ruler and a protractor.

1 a square with 5·7 cm sides

2 an equilateral triangle with 38 mm sides

3 a right-angled triangle with 30 degree and 60 degree angles

4 a rectangle with a perimeter of 24 cm

5 a rhombus with a 45 degree angle

5 Copy the blank division. Choose five digits from the oval to complete the division. Find the answer.

☐☐☐ ÷ ☐☐ = ______

1 2 4 7 5 8

Do this five times.

Which of your five divisions gives the answer nearest to 5·5?

Is there a better arrangement of the five digits that gives an answer nearer to 5·5?

Practice 22b

1 Copy these and write the missing numbers.

1	29 × ___ = 2929	2	___ × 630 = 1260	3	___ − 2700 = 2900
4	0·8 − ___ = 0·56	5	8200 − ___ = 4100	6	Half of ___ = 0·47
7	0·4 × ___ = 400	8	35^2 = ___	9	6690 − ___ = 379

2 Copy the calculations. Write brackets in each calculation to make it correct. You may wish to use a calculator.

1. 17 × 13 + 15 = 236
2. 259 − 138 ÷ 11 = 11
3. 47 + 86 × 93 − 55 = 5054
4. 129 − 72 ÷ 8 + 50 = 170

3 Write the measures in each box in order, smallest first.

3·7 m	3·07 m	7·3 m	7·03 m	0·73 m
2·14 kg	4·12 kg	1·4 kg	0·42 kg	1·24 kg
8·9 l	9·8 l	9·08 l	8·09 l	0·98 l
5·66 km	6·56 km	6·55 km	5·65 km	6·65 km

4 Write how many cubes each shape has.

1 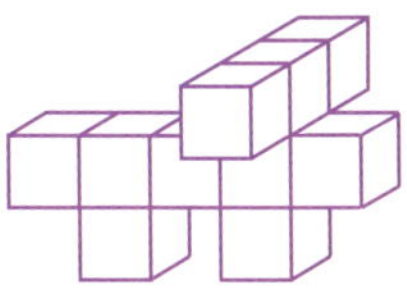

2 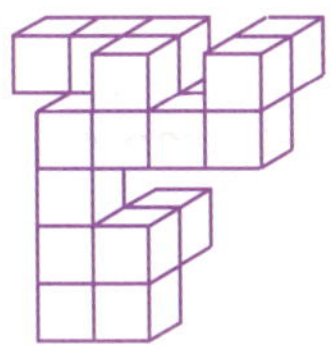

3 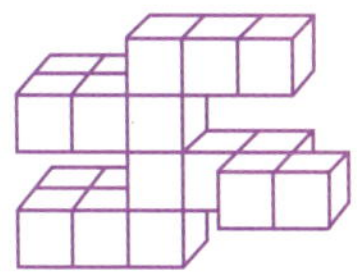

5 Choose the size of angles and the lengths of sides of the following shapes from the two boxes. You may use any of them more than once. Draw the shapes accurately.

1. a rectangle
2. a parallelogram
3. a rhombus
4. a right-angled isosceles triangle

30°	45°	60°
90°	120°	135°
	150°	

2·5 cm	3 cm
4 cm	6 cm
6·5 cm	9 cm

Practice 23a

1 Copy these and complete them.

1	63 + 65 + 67 = ____	2	1000 – 250 = ____	3	What is 20 squared?
4	Half of 0·58	5	7100 subtract 4800	6	23 × 101 = ____
7	6100 – 3800 = ____	8	17 + 17 = ____	9	0·94 × 1000 = ____

2 Copy and complete the grid.

Decimal number	0·92	0·88	2·67	9·13	0·11	7·48	0·75	5·55
Rounded to the nearest tenth								
Rounded to the nearest integer								

3 Copy these shapes on squared paper.

Circle each shape that is a net of a closed cube.

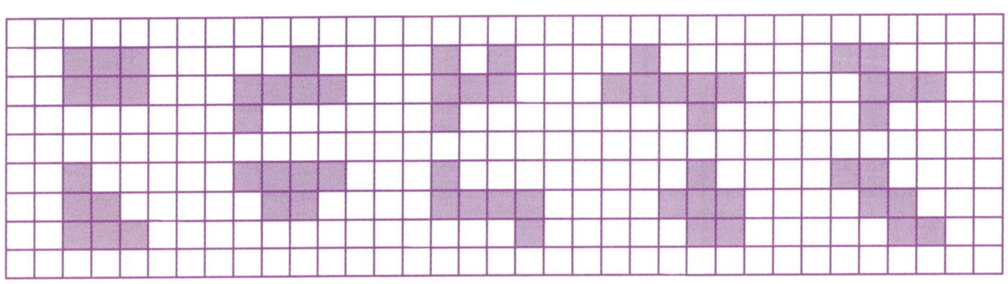

4 Order these angles, smallest first.

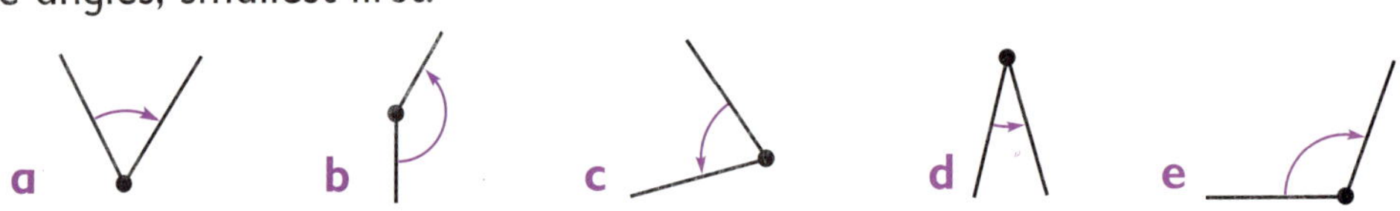

5 Draw a triangle on squared paper.

Rotate your triangle 90° clockwise about one corner. Draw the triangle in its new position.

Rotate your triangle 90° clockwise twice more, each time drawing it in its new position.

Do the same three times with a quadrilateral, a pentagon and a hexagon.

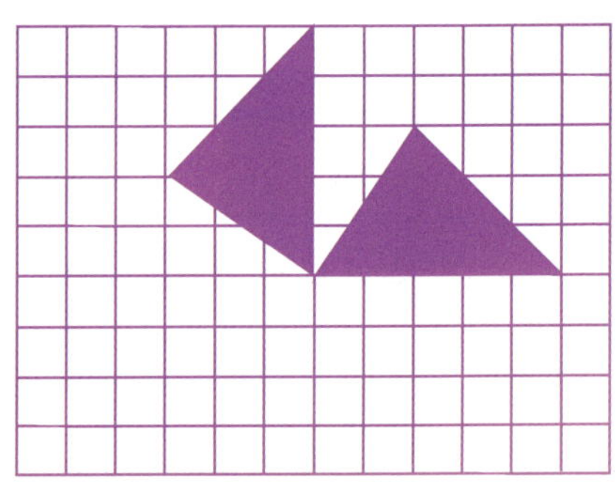

Practice 23b

1 Copy these and write the missing numbers.

1	713 ÷ ☐ = 23	2	☐ − 620 = 1240	3	☐ × 18 = 486
4	$\frac{3}{10}$ of ☐ = £9	5	800 + ☐ = 1600	6	☐ × 1000 = 730
7	Double ☐ = 720	8	4·7 × ☐ = 37·6	9	(☐ × 28) − 54 = 1150

2 Draw these shapes accurately. In each shape write 'a' in each acute angle, 'r' in each right angle and 'o' in each obtuse angle.

1

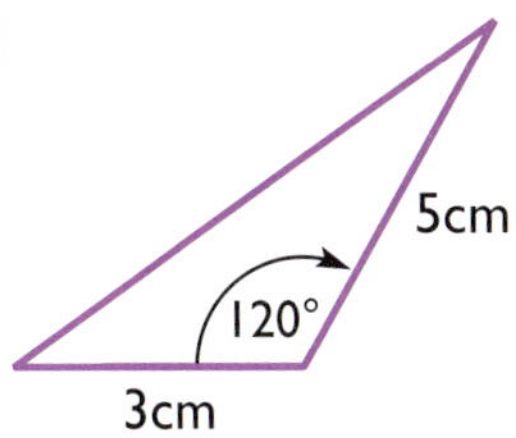

2

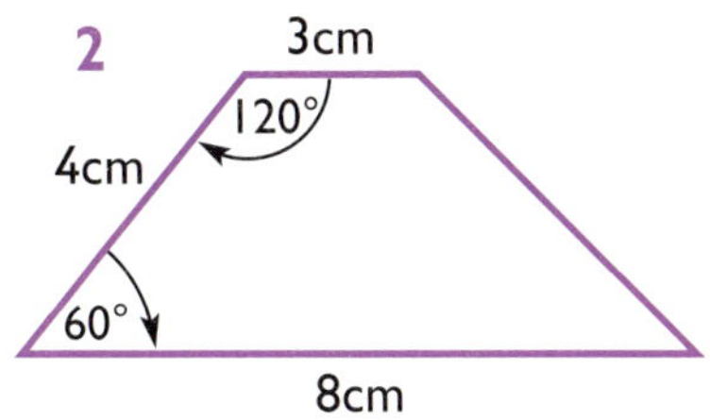

3

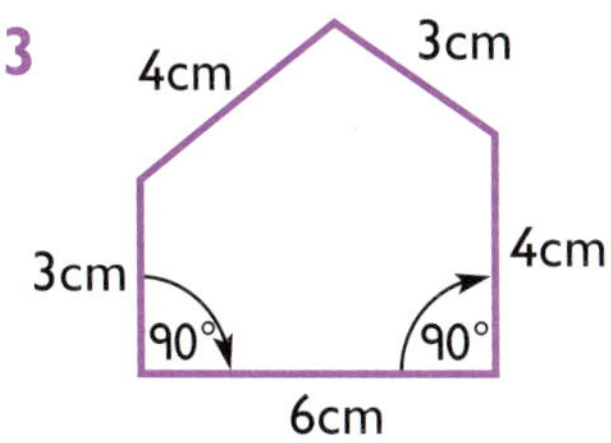

3 Copy the blank division. Choose five digits from the box to complete it. Work out the answer.

☐☐☐ ÷ ☐☐ = ______

Do this six times.

9	8	7	6	5
4	3	2	1	

4 Copy these triangles onto squared paper. Write about the translations and rotations that take each triangle to the next position.

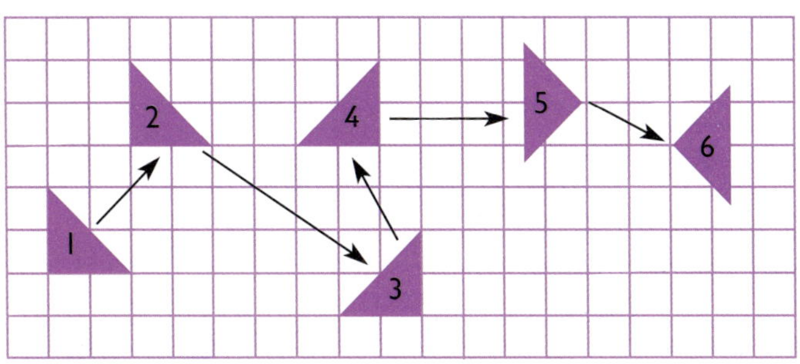

5 Investigate drawing two triangles whose sides intersect.

What can you say about the number of intersections?
What new shapes are formed?
Are the results different for different kinds of triangle?
Do the same with three triangles.

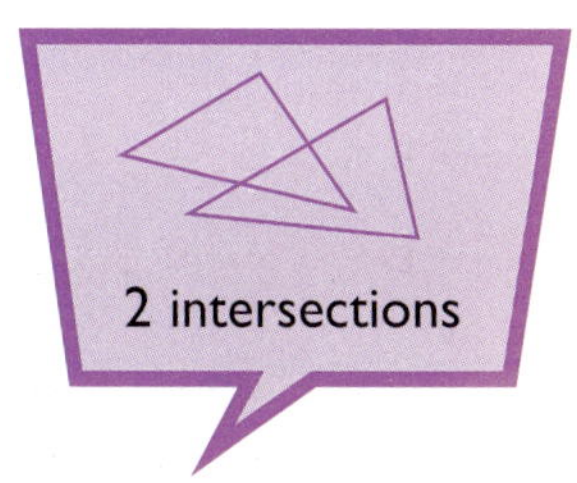

Practice 24a

1 Copy these and complete them.

1	$6{\cdot}7 \times 2{\cdot}9 =$ ____	2	$3{\cdot}9 \times 7 =$ ____	3	$0{\cdot}4 \times 10 =$ ____
4	$14 - (234 \div 18) =$ ____	5	Sum of 526 and 300	6	$1000 - 650 =$ ____
7	$23 \times 99 =$ ____	8	$400 + 400 =$ ____	9	$1 - 0{\cdot}6 =$ ____

2 Find these solid shapes in your classroom.

Write about the parallel and perpendicular lines in each solid. Making drawings may help.

3 Use squares and equilateral triangles to make each of the shapes in this sequence.

Draw the shapes.

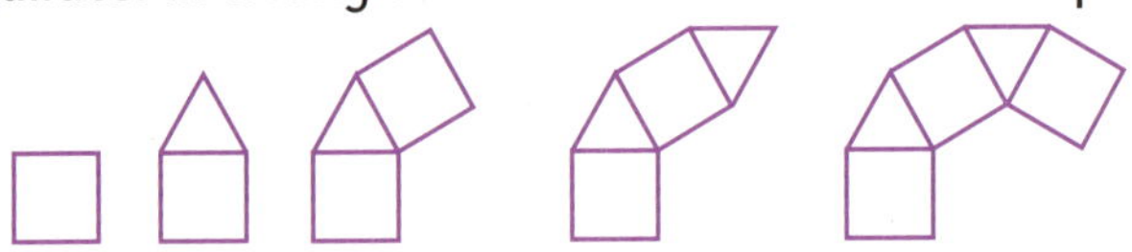

Make and then draw the next two and the last shape in the sequence.

4 Copy and complete the table. Use a protractor to help you.

angle	acute or obtuse	number of degrees
a		
b		
c		
d		
e		

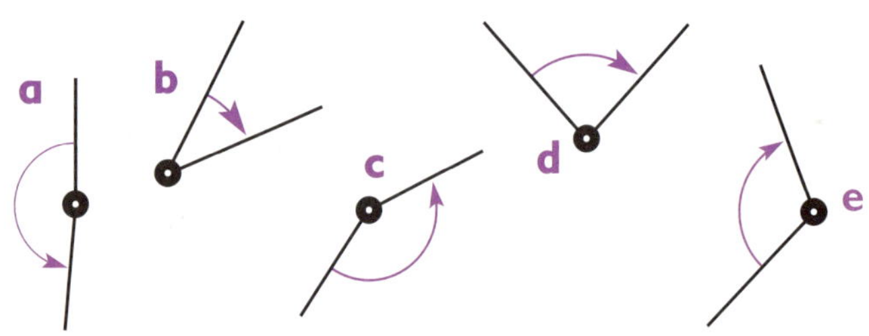

5 Draw a triangle. Label the angles *a*, *b* and *c*.

Draw three more triangles.

Copy and complete the table.

Write about the sum of the three angles.

triangle	size of angle a	size of angle b	size of angle c	sum of a, b, and c
1				
2				
3				
4				

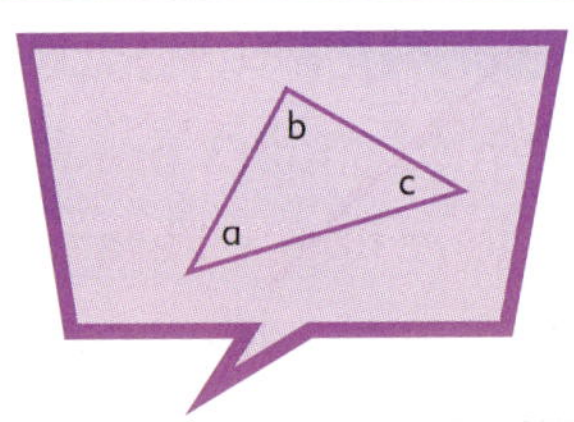

Practice 24b

1 Copy these and write the missing numbers.

1	0·7 + □ = 1	2	□ + 7·59 = 7·6	3	□ × 100 = 80
4	□ − 70 = 70	5	□ × 99 = 2871	6	6^2 − □ = 4^2
7	□ − 0·31 = 0·22	8	□ ÷ 6 = 32·7	9	37 × □ = 925

2 Draw these shapes. On each shape mark the angles as acute or obtuse.

1 A triangle with two acute and one obtuse angle.

2 A quadrilateral with three acute and one obtuse angle.

3 A quadrilateral with two acute and two obtuse angles.

4 A quadrilateral with one acute and three obtuse angles.

Is it possible to draw a triangle with more than one obtuse angle? Explain.

Is it possible to draw a quadrilateral with four obtuse angles? Explain.

3 Copy and complete the statements.

1	1·01 kg = □ g	2	0·11 kg = □ g	3	1·1 kg = □ g
4	10·1 kg = □ g	5	0·101 kg = □ g	6	0·011 kg = □ g

4 Copy the recipe for shortbread biscuits.

Rewrite the recipe using grams rounded to the nearest 5 grams. The conversion line may help you.

10 oz plain flour
2 oz ground rice
$7\frac{1}{2}$ oz butter
$3\frac{1}{2}$ oz caster sugar

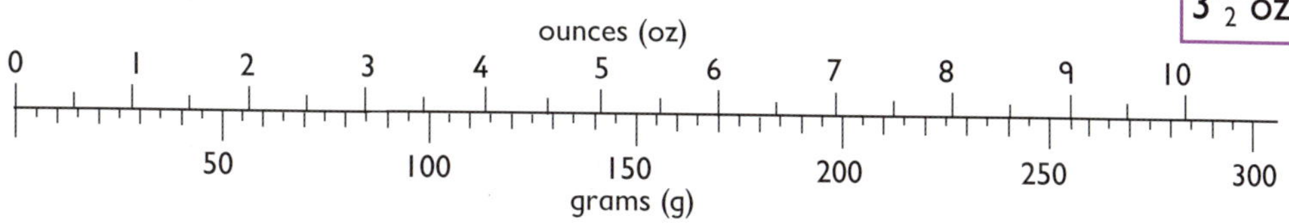

5 Draw three lines that meet at a point. Measure and record each of the three angles at the point.

Find the sum of the three angles.
Do this three times.

Do this again for four and then five lines at a point.
What can you say about the sum of the angles?

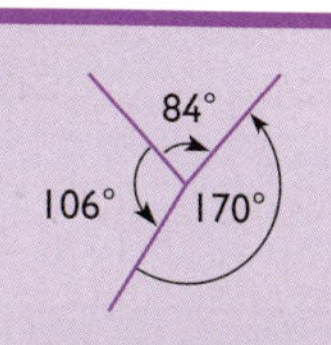

84° + 106° + 170° = 360°

Practice 25a

1 Copy these and complete them.

1	5361 – 3150 = ____	**2**	100 – 29 = ____	**3**	68 × 6 = ____
4	4·6 – 2·9 = ____	**5**	154 – 77 = ____	**6**	6 take away 5·3
7	What is the square of 25?	**8**	86 + 86 = ____	**9**	8400 – 5600 = ____

2 Copy the shape onto centimetre-squared paper.

Find the area of each shaded rectangle.

What is the total of the shaded area?

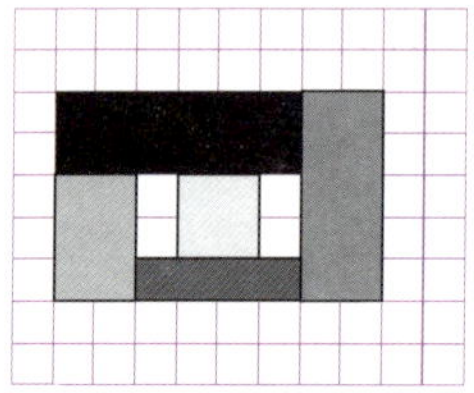

3 Copy the incomplete statement. Choose two numbers from the box to complete the statement.

☐ grams = ☐ kilograms

Repeat for six more pairs of numbers.

1000 0·25 0·2 1 100 10 200 0·5 250 0·75 750 500 0·1 0·01

4 Copy and complete the multiplications.

1	8 × 7 = ____	**2**	3 × 7 = ____
3	10 × 7 = ____	**4**	5 × 7 = ____

Copy the axes on graph paper, extending the y-axis further.

Plot the products. Complete the 'multiplication by 7' line graph.

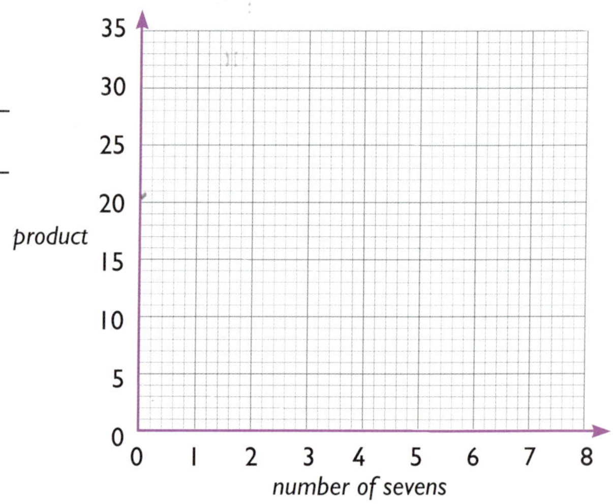

5 Copy the subtraction. Choose three digits from the circle to complete it.

9	0	0		–		9	9	

Work out the answer.

Repeat for six sets of three digits.

1 3 5 7 6 8

Practice 25b

1 Copy these and write the missing numbers.

1	☐ + 0·9 = 3·7	2	399 ÷ ☐ = 21	3	6262 + ☐ = 8061
4	☐ + 1400 = 2800	5	1400 – ☐ = 700	6	9·9 × ☐ = 9900
7	Double ☐ = 1520	8	☐ – 2·1 = 5·5	9	☐ – (35 × 19) = 1

2 Calculate the area of each rectangle. The rectangles are not to scale.

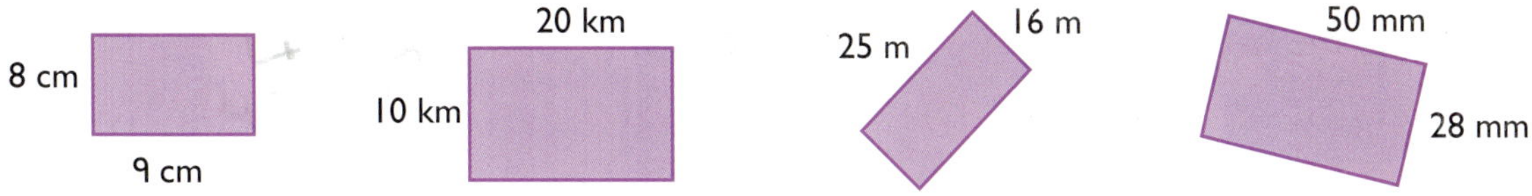

3

1 How many 747s nose to tail would stretch as far as the length of the SkyCat?

2 The weight of a 747 is about 330 000 kg. How many 747s could a SkyCat carry?

3 What is the ratio of the 747's payload to that of the SkyCat?

4 What percentage of the height of the SkyCat is the 747?

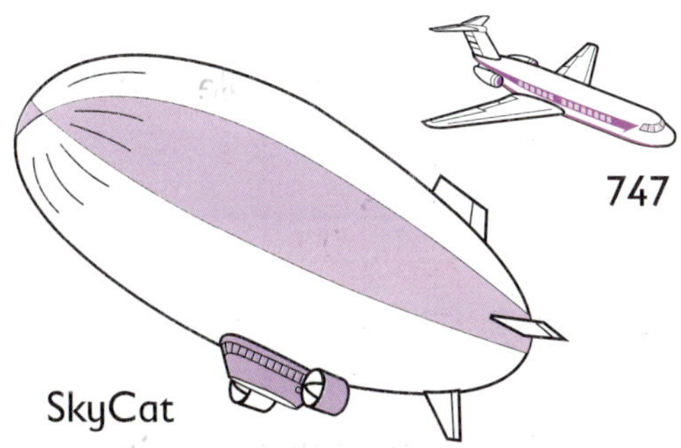

	747	SkyCat
length	70 m	307 m
height	19 m	77 m
payload	61000 kg	1 million kg
speed	584 mph	120 mph

4 Measure the size of each angle. Draw the angles accurately.

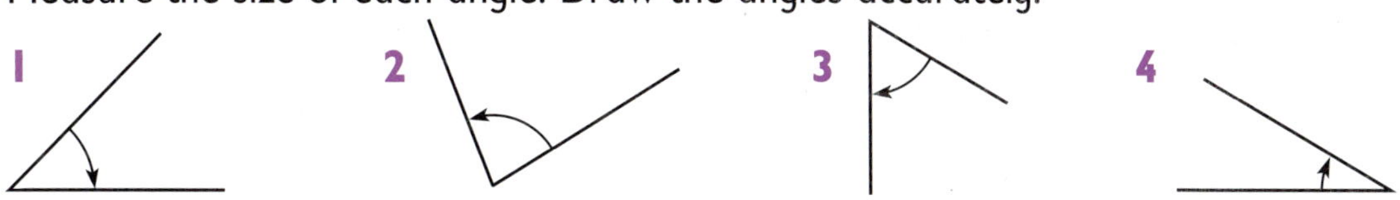

5 The same letters represent the same digit.

Find what each letter represents.

```
  R I G H T
+ R I G H T
  W R O N G
```

Practice 26a

1 Copy these and complete them.

1 $1102 \div 38 =$ ____ 2 $2124 + 2453 =$ ____ 3 $135{\cdot}6 + 8{\cdot}55 =$ ____

4 $6{\cdot}4 \times 100 =$ ____ 5 $50 \div 1000 =$ ____ 6 Total 320 and 158

7 Double 0·8 8 $7{\cdot}3 + 1{\cdot}1 =$ ____ 9 Divide 126 by 9

2 How much does the flour on each set of scales weigh?

1
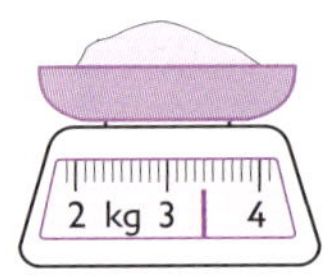

2

3

3 Copy the two blank numbers. Choose seven digits from the box to complete the numbers.

1	2	3	4	5	6	7	8	9

☐☐☐☐ ☐☐☐

Find the sum and the difference of the two numbers.

Do this four times.

4 Use Nyla's rule to find the area of these rectangles.

1 2 cm × 8 cm 2 12 m × 30 m 3 4 km × 9 km

How would Nyla's rule work on a 20 m × 1 km rectangle?

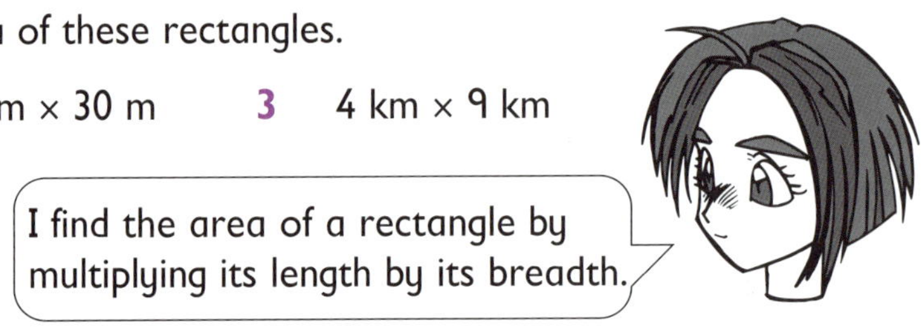

5 Copy the incomplete statements. Choose digits from the box to complete the statements. You may use a digit more than once.

1	2	3	4	5	6	7	8	9

Double 0·☐☐ = 0·☐☐

Double 0·☐☐ = 1·☐☐

Do this six times.

Practice 26b

1 Copy these and write the missing numbers.

1	6002 − ☐ = 3017	2	3900 + ☐ = 7800	3	☐ ÷ 39 = 27
4	4750 + ☐ = 6883	5	☐ − 5·31 = 147·96	6	☐ − 68 = 68
7	4·7 + ☐ = 6·6	8	25 × ☐ = 925	9	(448 ÷ 16) + ☐ = 100

2 Copy the plan of the garden. All the lengths are in metres. Calculate the area of each vegetable plot and the lawn.

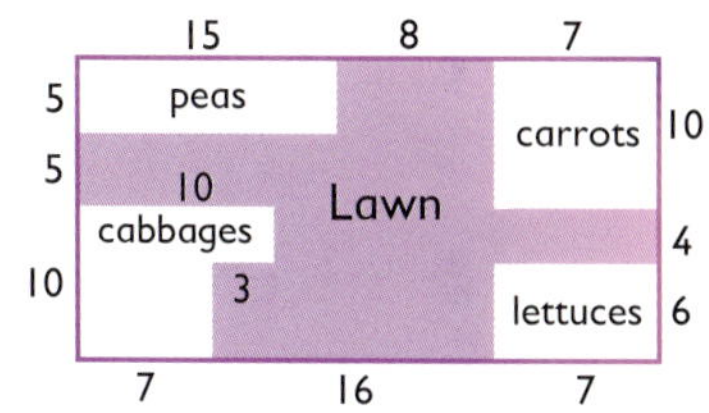

3 Copy and complete the subtractions. Counting up from the smaller number to the larger may help.

1 6000 − 3992 = ______ 2 4000 − 1895 = ______

3 8000 − 6780 = ______ 4 5003 − 2879 = ______

4 Copy the blank decimal number. Use three digits from the circle to complete the number.

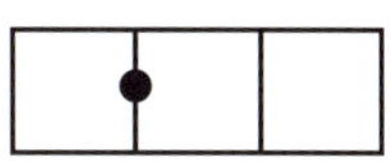

Make five numbers this way.

Find the differences between four different pairs of your numbers.

$$\begin{array}{r} 4{\cdot}19 \\ -\ 1{\cdot}74 \\ \hline 2{\cdot}45 \end{array}$$

5 Copy the calculations. Find the operations, + or −, hidden behind the clouds.

1 1 ☁ 2 ☁ 34 ☁ 5 ☁ 67 ☁ 8 ☁ 9 = 100

2 12 ☁ 3 ☁ 4 ☁ 5 ☁ 67 ☁ 8 ☁ 9 = 100

3 123 ☁ 4 ☁ 5 ☁ 6 ☁ 7 ☁ 8 ☁ 9 = 100

4 123 ☁ 4 ☁ 5 ☁ 67 ☁ 89 = 100

5 123 ☁ 45 ☁ 67 ☁ 89 = 100

Practice 27a

1 Copy these and complete them.

1	1430 – 730 = ____	2	67 + (425 ÷ 17) = ____	3	3·5 – 1·1 = ____
4	360 × 2 = ____	5	8609 – 5207 = ____	6	0·13 × 10 = ____
7	Share 104 among 8	8	463·2 – 6·48 = ____	9	Take 1·1 from 2

2

1. The Hungarian Grand Prix race has 77 laps. How long is the race?
2. A car breaks down after 0·73 of the first lap. How far is the driver from completing the first lap?
3. The race is abandoned because of heavy rain. The winner has completed 53 laps and is 9·32 miles ahead of the second car. How far has the second car travelled when the race is ended?

The Hungaroring, Mogyorod, Hungary

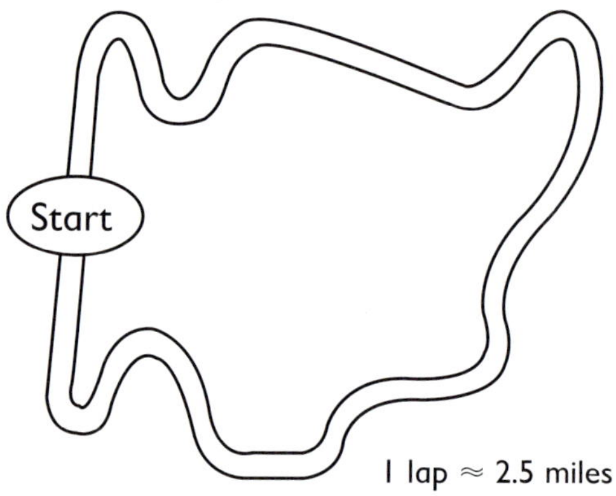

3

1	3·6 + 17·5 = ☐	2	8·29 + 14·8 = ☐	3	0·86 + 5·95 = ☐
4	49·08 + 13·95 = ☐	5	6·47 + 18·6 = ☐	6	20·66 + 39·55 = ☐

4 Copy the calculations. The answers are incorrect as two digits are in the wrong position each time. Use a calculator to find which ones are wrong.

1. 39 504 + 48 095 = 89 579
2. 378 × 46 = 17 838
3. 60 207 – 13 948 = 56 249
4. 16 060 ÷ 55 = 922

5 Copy the incomplete calculation. Choose two operations from the box to replace the stars.

+	–	×	÷

You may use the same operation twice.

Work out the answer.

14 976 ★ 312 ★ 16 =

Do this six times.

Practice 27b

1 Copy these and write the missing numbers.

1 □ + 7600 = 15 200 2 6·33 + □ = 6·4 3 □ + 3146 = 8558

4 □ × 40 = 12 5 Double □ = 2800 6 □ + 2·9 = 12·3

7 □ + 6·12 = 133·5 8 60 – □ = 30 9 1053 ÷ □ = 39

2 Copy the additions and work out the answers.

1 45 + 9 + 18 + 13 = ______ 2 13 + 18 + 9 + 45 = ______

What do you notice about the two additions?

Which is the better order to add the numbers? Explain why.

Find a better order to add these.

3 29 + 5 + 17 + 36 ______ 4 9 + 62 + 11 + 24 ______

3

1 How many more straws are there in the large packet than the other two packets put together?

2 How many small packets does Jack need to buy to have the same number as is in the large packet?

3 Ayesha buys 875 straws in a combination of different packets. How many of each packet does she buy?

4 Copy the number grid and shade the prime numbers.

1	2	3	4	5
6	7	8	9	10
11	12	13	14	15
16	17	18	19	20

5 What could the numbers be?

1 It is between 10 and 30 and is a multiple of 7.

2 It is between 30 and 60 and is a multiple of 13.

3 It is between 60 and 80 and is a multiple of 8.

4 It is between 40 and 90 and is a multiple of 17.

Practice 28a

1 Copy these and complete them.

1	0·46 + 0·5 = ____	2	74 ÷ 100 = ____	3	76 × 4 = ____
4	Increase 4900 by 1400	5	4506 + 1272 = ____	6	7·94 + 86·6
7	520 + 520 = ____	8	187 × 2 = ____	9	92 × 100 = ____

2

1 Leyla buys 5 trays of petunias. How much change will she get from a £20 note?

2 Greg pays £55.60 for potted roses. How many plants does he buy?

3 Iain has £30 to spend. What could he buy so that he is left with less than £1?

4 Bridget spends £40.75 on some of each. How many of each does she buy?

3 Copy and complete the prime factor diagrams.

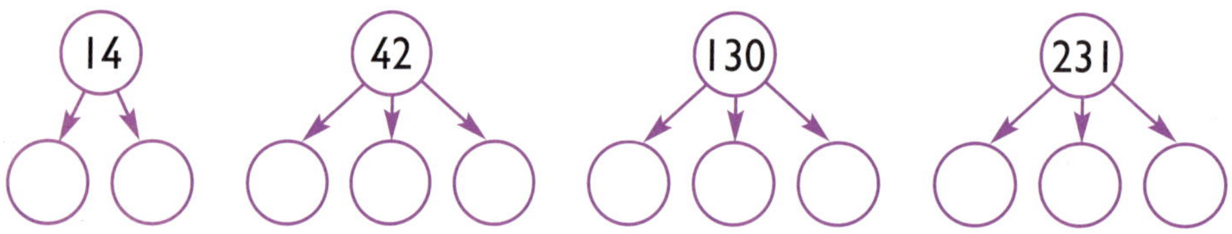

4 Copy the sorting grid. Sort the numbers in the box in the correct places.

	multiples of 3	multiples of 7
multiples of 2		
multiples of 5		

6	98	36
175	15	35
12	90	14

5 Copy the incomplete statements. Choose digits from the box to complete the statements. You may use a digit more than once.

1	2	3	4	5	6	7	8	9

Half of | 0 • | | | = | 0 • | | |

Half of | 1 • | | | = | 0 • | | |

Do this six times.

Practice 28b

1 Copy these and write the missing numbers.

1	4·5 + □ = 10	2	□ − 27 = 27	3	28·67 − □ = 18·97
4	2·34 + □ = 2·4	5	□ − 2987 = 2013	6	0·63 × □ = 6·3
7	□ ÷ 7 = 3·1	8	8·15 + □ = 85·95	9	(□ ÷ 24) − 19 = 20

2 Copy the counter sequences. Draw the next three shapes in each sequence.

Write a formula for the number of counters in the *n*th number in each sequence.

1
2
3

3 Give three examples of products with a different number of even numbers each time.

Write general statements about:

1 the product of any number of odd numbers

2 the product of any number of odd and even numbers.

Give three examples for each general statement.

4 Copy the four incomplete decimal multiplications. Use all the digits 0 to 9 to complete the four multiplications. Find the answers.

□•□ × 10 = ______ □•□ × 100 = ______

□•□□ × 10 = ______ □•□□ × 100 = ______

Do this four times.

5 Investigate shapes that can be made using 3 squares.

Write a rule for restricting the number of possible shapes.

Suggest how to extend the investigation by copying and completing this sentence.

'If instead of squares we used ...'

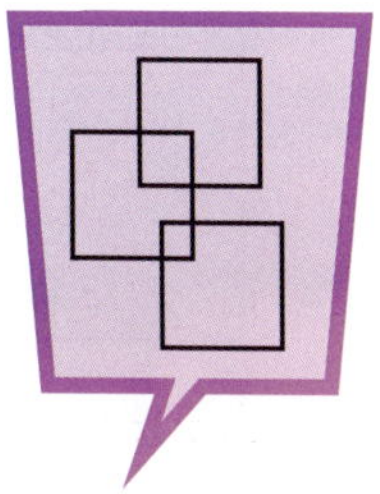

Practice 29a

1 Copy these and complete them.

1	$3 \div 100 =$ ____	2	$2{\cdot}5 + 2{\cdot}1 =$ ____	3	$0{\cdot}15 \times 2 =$ ____
4	Add 3·7 to 1·8	5	$0{\cdot}8 + 0{\cdot}2 =$ ____	6	$(36 \times 12) + 59 =$ ____
7	$15{\cdot}75 - 9{\cdot}6 =$ ____	8	$2300 + 2300 =$ ____	9	$0{\cdot}03 + 0{\cdot}8 =$ ____

2 For each statement give three examples to show that it is either true or false.

1 The product of two odd numbers is odd.

2 The product of three odd numbers is odd.

3 The product of an even and an odd number is odd.

3 Copy the two dot sequences and draw the next three shapes hidden under the clouds.

1 

2 

4 Copy the calculations and work out the answers. Explain how you did each one.

1	$350 + 351 =$ ____	2	$900\,000 - 899\,989 =$ ____
3	$54 \times 22 =$ ____	4	$899 \div 29 =$ ____

5 Copy the Venn diagram. Choose two numbers from the circle for the empty boxes. Write two of your own numbers on each region of the diagram.

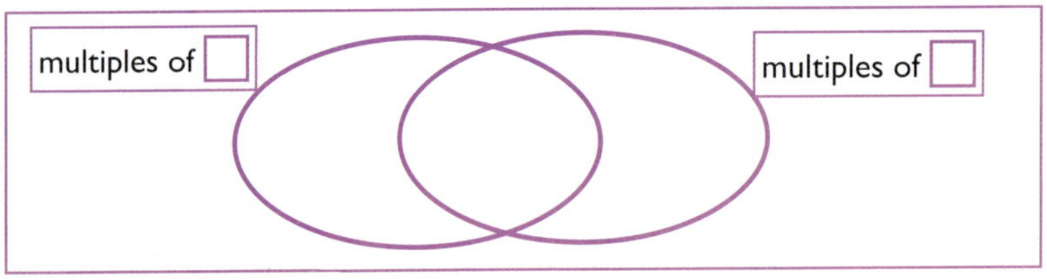

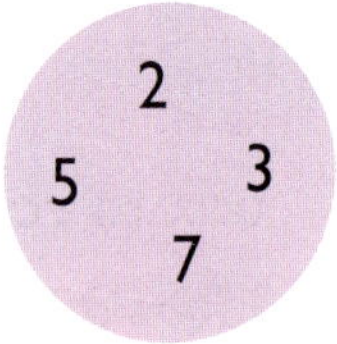

Do this for six pairs of numbers.

Practice 29b

1 Copy these and write the missing numbers.

1	☐ + 2·6 = 10	2	104 − ☐ = 52	3	☐ × 10 = 31·3
4	8 × ☐ = 2·4	5	6·4 ÷ ☐ = 0·8	6	3·5 + ☐ = 4·6
7	☐ − 4132 = 5458	8	Double ☐ = 5400	9	☐ × 15 = 240

2 Find three examples to match each general statement.

1 The sum of four consecutive numbers is even.

2 A multiple of 6 is also a multiple of 3.

3 The difference of two consecutive square numbers is an odd number.

4 The opposite angles in a parallelogram are equal.

3 Estimate the numbers the arrows are pointing to.

1 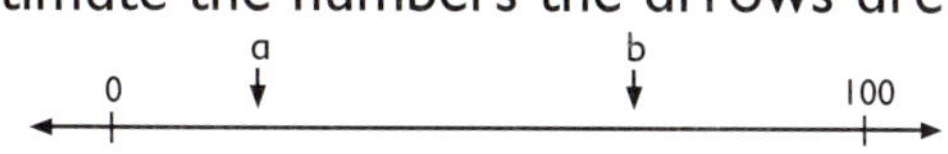

2 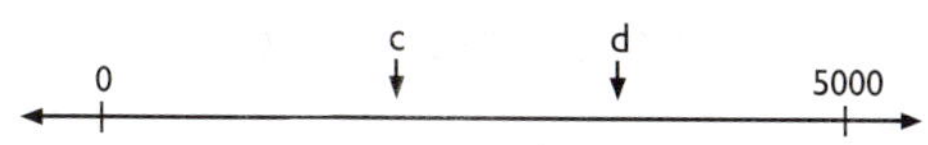

3 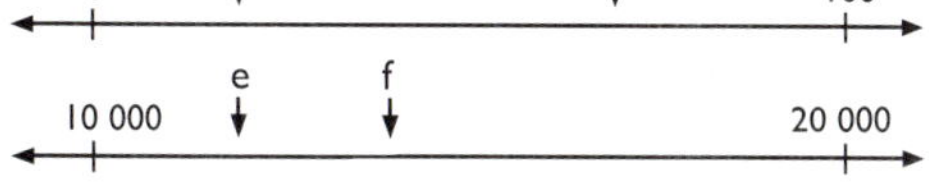

4 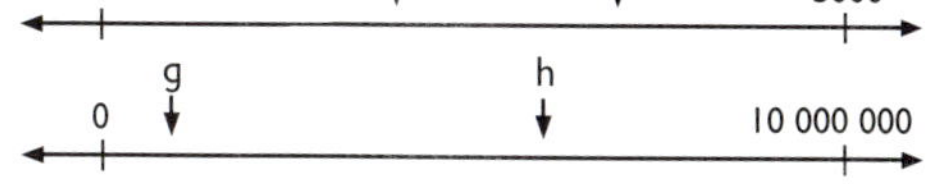

4 In each pair estimate the size of the unmarked object.

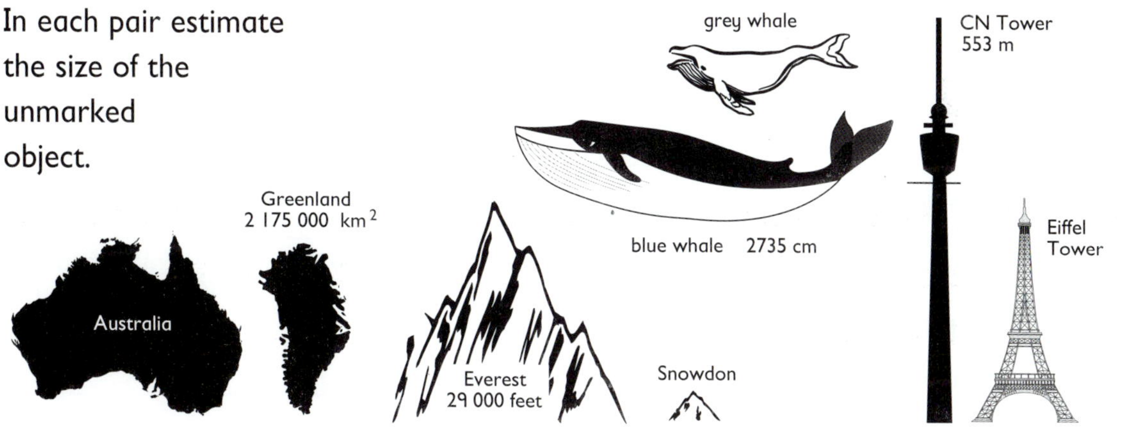

5 Copy the blank fraction. Choose two numbers from the box to complete a proper or an improper fraction.

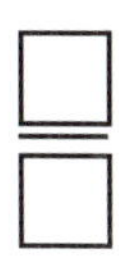

3	6	9	11	7	13

$\frac{7}{3} \approx 2{\cdot}3333333$
$\approx 2{\cdot}33$

Change the fraction to a decimal, writing the decimal to the nearest hundredth. A calculator may be useful. Do this six times.

Practice 30a

1 Copy these and complete them.

1	0·8 × 4 = _____	2	6·7 – 2·1 = _____	3	5·7 + 4·3 = _____
4	6400 – 3200 = _____	5	596 – (23 × 19) = _____	6	4·9 × 6 = _____
7	60% of £50	8	6 × 1000 = _____	9	Subtract 3·82 from 3·9

2 Copy the grid. Ring the number for which the statement is a divisibility test.

Divisibility test	Appropriate number							
the last digit is 0 or a 5	2	3	4	5	6	8	9	10
the last digit is even	2	3	4	5	6	8	9	10
the number is even and is divisible by 3	2	3	4	5	6	8	9	10
the sum of the digits is divisible by 3	2	3	4	5	6	8	9	10

3 Estimate the number of marbles in the second container in each pair.

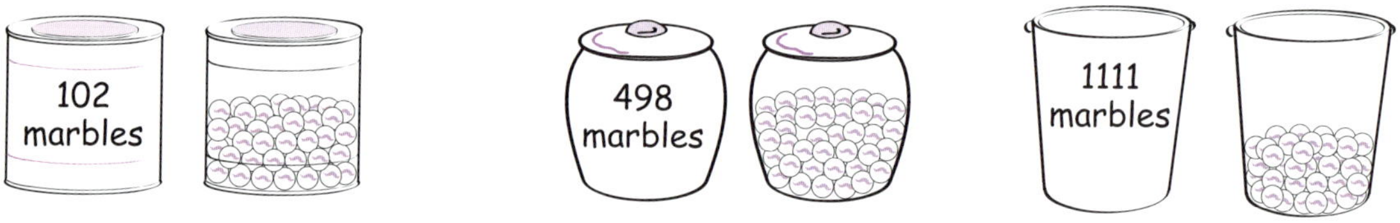

4 Copy the grid. Write each quotient as a mixed number and a decimal. A calculator may help you. Where appropriate write a decimal to the nearest hundredth.

quotient	7 ÷ 2	11 ÷ 3	29 ÷ 4	19 ÷ 5	37 ÷ 6	54 ÷ 7	91 ÷ 8	65 ÷ 9
mixed number	$3\frac{1}{2}$							
decimal	3·5							

5 Write three multiplications which match what Shazad says.

Write three multiplications that do *not* match what Shazad says.

Investigate patterns in the unit digits of the product of two consecutive numbers.

Practice 30b

1 Copy these and write the missing numbers.

1	8·6 + □ = 11·7	2	□ − 5·31 = 147·9	3	□ × 100 = 280
4	□ × 32 = 4576	5	7927 − □ = 5312	6	□ ÷ 6 = 4·5
7	1 − □ = 0·5	8	0·36 × □ = 0·18	9	69 − (□ ÷ 41) = 50

2

1. About 1500 tonnes of salt and sand was stored ready for putting on icy roads. Nearly three-quarters of it was used. Estimate how much was left.
2. Approximately two-thirds of the 400 wasps in a nest were killed with a spray. About how many were still alive?
3. In a gale, nearly thirty-five per cent of a plantation of 2890 trees were destroyed. About how many trees were left?

3 Copy and complete the grid.

number	978 362	705 058	493 045	123 456	876 543
rounded to nearest 1000					
rounded to nearest 10 000					
rounded to nearest 100 000					

4 Copy the four divisions. Use six of the digits 1 to 9 to complete the divisions. Find the answers.

□□ ÷ 10 = ______   □□ ÷ 100 = ______

□ ÷ 10 = ______   □ ÷ 100 = ______

Repeat with six different sets of digits.

5 Copy the incomplete two-digit by one-digit multiplication.

□□ × □ = 504

How many different solutions can you find?

Do this again for the answers 288, 396 and 450.

84 × 6 = 504

Practice 31a

1 Copy these and complete them.

1	4·9 + 3·1 = ____	2	27 + (27 × 27) = ____	3	7·5 subtract 7·43
4	25% of £200	5	0·6 × 7 = ____	6	Sum of 0·78 and 0·27
7	80% of 5 litres	8	283·1 + 7·8 = ____	9	11800 – 5900 = ____

2 Write the number each arrow is pointing to.

1 a ⟶ –3

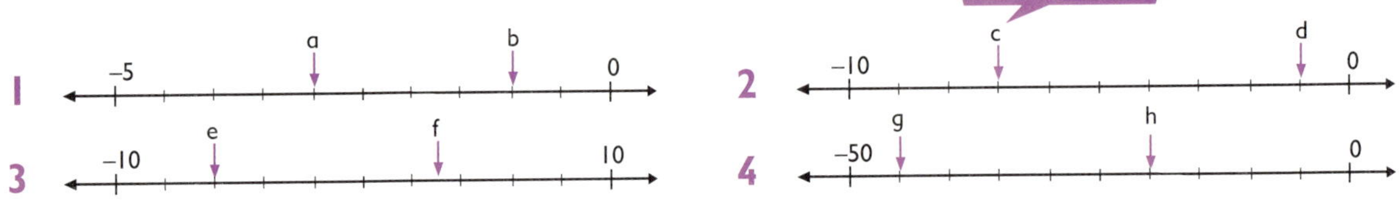

3 Copy and complete the approximation diagram by following the arrows.

Draw diagrams to find approximations for 59 × 31 and 88 × 68. Choose the best way to round each number.

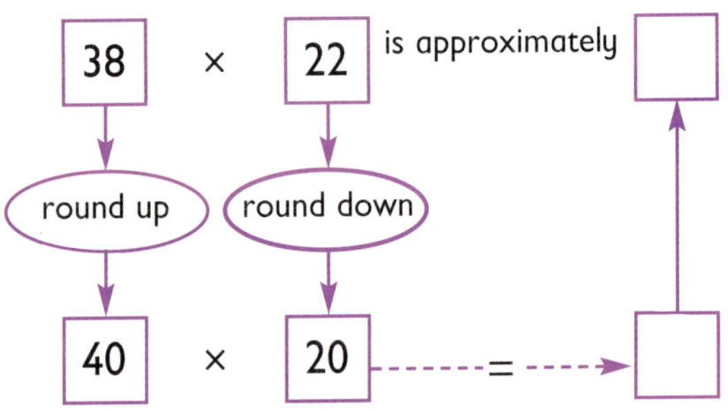

4 You may wish to use a calculator to work out these calculations.

1 (37 + 51) × (76 + 23) = ______

2 (529 + 1865) ÷ (1248 – 1191) = ______

3 19 × (438 + 297) – 13 458 = ______

5 Copy the incomplete multiplications. Choose three digits from the box to complete each one. A digit can be used more than once.

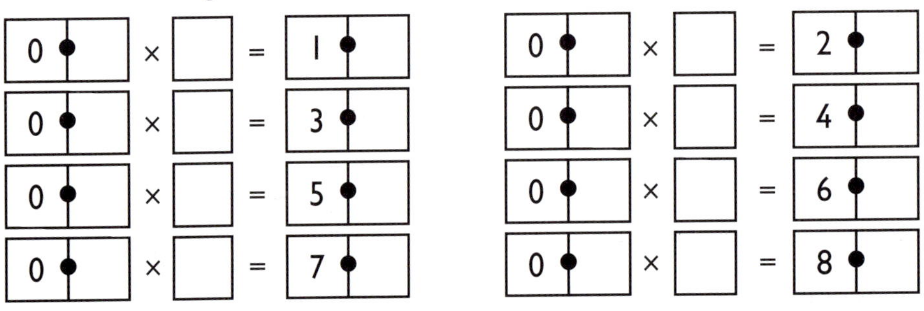

1 2 3 4 5 6 7 8 9

Practice 31b

1 Copy these and write the missing numbers.

1	☐ × 4 = 15·2	2	☐ − 0·9 = 7·4	3	☐ % of £10 = £3
4	Double ☐ = 11800	5	$\frac{21}{100}$ of ☐ = 63 km	6	☐ + 4·91 = 5
7	☐ − 0·2 = 0·88	8	20% of ☐ = 6 m	9	6 ÷ ☐ = 0·6

2 Estimate the decimal numbers the arrows are pointing to.

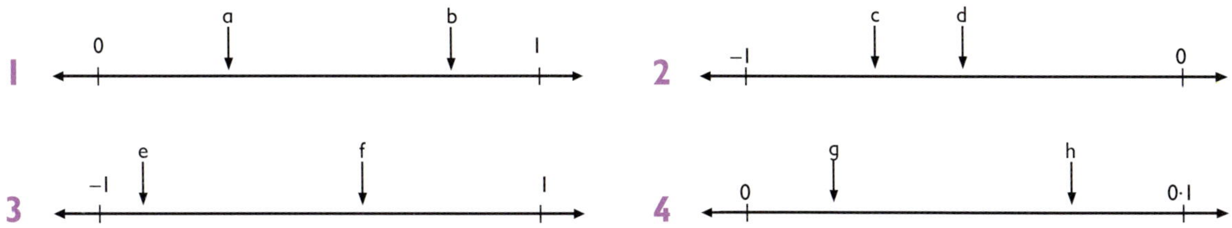

3

1 In the world the ratio of Muslims to Christians is 1 to 2. There are about 2000 million Christians. Approximately how many Muslims are there?

2 In Britain there is one doctor for every 700 people. The population is 60 million. About how many doctors are there?

3 In Russia there are about 10 million more women than men and for every 8 women there are 7 men. About how many people live in Russia?

4 Copy and complete the grid. A calculator may be helpful.

division	579 ÷ 4	1000 ÷ 3	7000 ÷ 6	41832 ÷ 7	30303 ÷ 2
answer					
rounded to nearest 100					
rounded to nearest 10					

5 Copy the diagram. Choose any percentage. Write it in the percentage sector. Write the fraction and the decimal that are equivalent to your percentage in their sectors.

Do this three times.

Do it again starting with a fraction.

Do it again starting with a decimal.

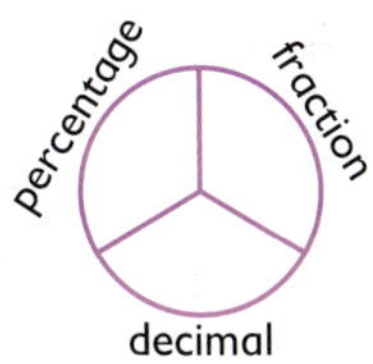

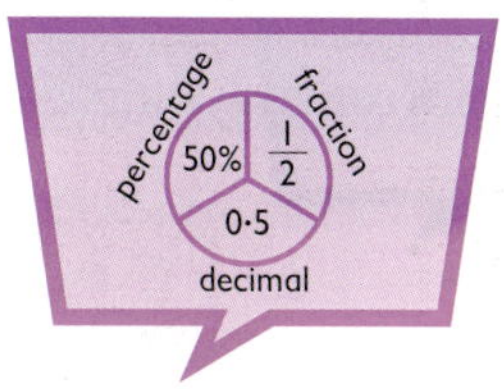

Practice 32a

1 Copy these and complete them.

1	5·4 – 3·1 = ____	2	10% of 1 kg	3	6·7 × 100 = ____
4	From 0·9 take 0·52	5	50% of £7	6	0·35 ÷ 2 = ____
7	$\frac{3}{5}$ of 100 = ____	8	4700 + 4700 = ____	9	30·48 – 2·49 = ____

2

1 A glass is filled with 150 millilitres using a full 2-litre bottle of lemonade. How much is left in the bottle?

2 In a triathlon, Amanda swims 500 metres, cycles 12 kilometres and runs for 1·5 kilometres. How far is the triathlon altogether?

3 Tino makes a vegetarian dish. He uses 2 kg of potatoes, 1·5 kg of carrots, 700 g of cauliflower and 250 g of peas. How much do the vegetables weigh in total?

3 Copy the incomplete calculation. Choose a fraction from the box and a number from the oval to complete it.

Work out the answer.

$\frac{\square}{\square}$ of $\square$ = ▒

$\frac{1}{10}$ $\frac{3}{10}$ $\frac{7}{100}$

100 500 1000

$\frac{1}{10}$ of 100 = 10

Do this six times.

4

1 A town of 20 000 people is hit by a hurricane. 9 in every 10 people are left homeless. How many people are without homes?

2 In parts of Java there is a thunderstorm 2 days in every 3. About how many days in a year does it thunder?

3 Did you know that a hibernating hedgehog breathes only once every 6 seconds? How many times does a hibernating hedgehog breathe in 1 hour?

5 Copy the two statements.

Choose any nine digits to make them correct. A digit may be used more than once.

$\frac{\square}{1000}$ = 0·$\square\square\square$ $\frac{\square\square}{1000}$ = 0·$\square\square\square$

Practice 32b

1 Copy these and write the missing numbers.

1	60% of ☐ = £4.80	2	1000 – ☐ = 850	3	5·7 – ☐ = 3·8
4	4·8 × ☐ = 480	5	☐ × 2 = 0·5	6	8·38 + ☐ = 9
7	☐ of 72 = 9	8	☐ ÷ 100 = 0·26	9	☐ % of 4 km = 2·8 km

2 Copy and complete the diagram. Explain how the diagram helps to find an approximation to 47 × 34.

Draw similar diagrams to find approximations to:

59 × 63   82 × 28   77 × 96

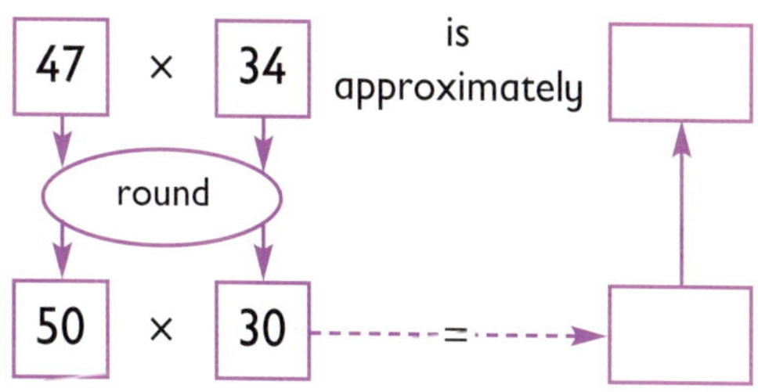

3 Copy the two boxes. Match a fraction to its equivalent decimal. A calculator may be helpful. Be careful as some decimals have been rounded to the nearest thousandth.

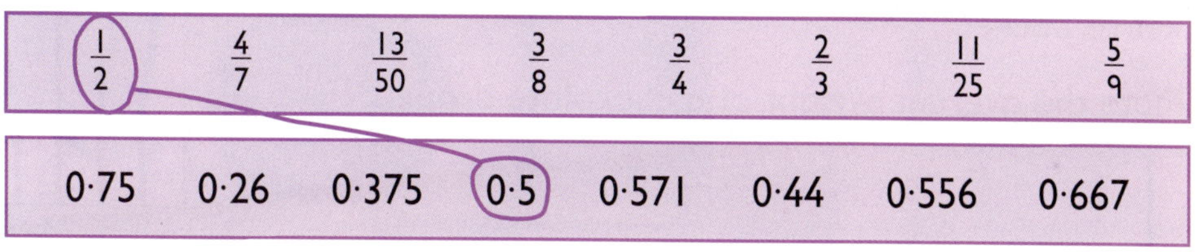

4

1 The largest meteorite to land on Earth came down in Namibia. It weighed 60 tonnes. The next largest which weighed 30 tonnes landed in Greenland. What fraction of 60 tonnes is 30 tonnes?

2 The planet Mercury is approximately 58 million kilometres from the Sun while the Earth is about 150 million kilometres from the Sun. Write 58 million kilometres as a fraction of 150 million kilometres.

3 Everest is 29 000 feet high. Ben Nevis is 4408 feet high. What fraction of the height of Everest is Ben Nevis?

5 Copy the blank decimal number. Choose any four digits to complete it. Write a mixed number and an improper fraction that are equivalent to the decimal number. Do this six times.

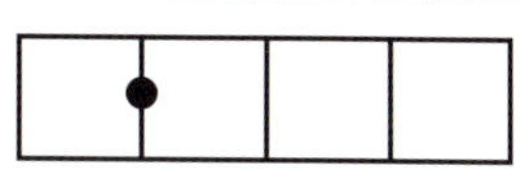

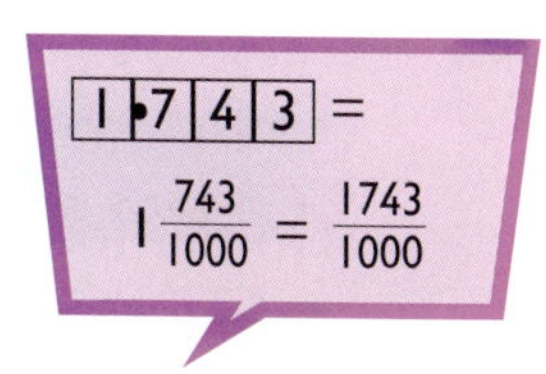

Practice 33a

1 Copy these and complete them.

1	$0{\cdot}81 + 0{\cdot}3 =$ ____	2	$\frac{7}{10}$ of 70 = ____	3	$(48 \times 16) - 123 =$ ____
4	$0{\cdot}75 \times 2 =$ ____	5	$\frac{1}{6}$ of 12 kg	6	$0{\cdot}5 - 0{\cdot}12 =$ ____
7	Add 0·08 to 0·4	8	30% of £9	9	$720 \div 100 =$ ____

2 Copy these and complete them.

1	5 m = ☐ cm	2	0·8 m = ☐ mm	3	2·4 km = ☐ m
4	3·29 cm = ☐ mm	5	0·392 km = ☐ m	6	0·6 cm = ☐ mm

3

1 How many packets were used for the survey?

2 What was the most frequent number of chocolate drops in a packet?

3 Explain why the number of drops varies from packet to packet.

4 Estimate the average weight of a chocolate drop.

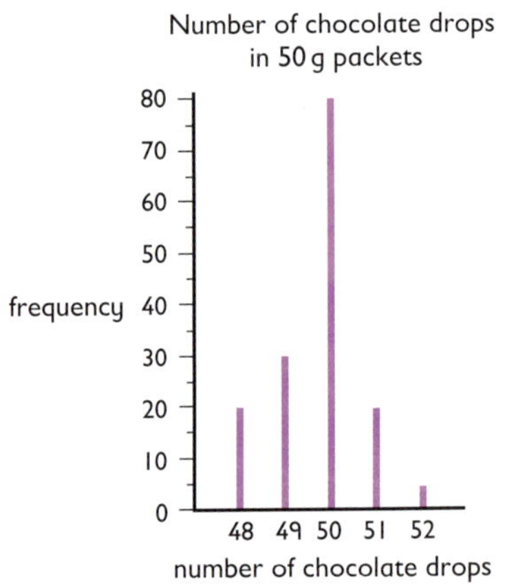

4 Copy and complete the calculations.

1	100% of £400 = ☐	2	50% of 700 km = ☐	3	50% of 200 kg = ☐
	50% of £400 = ☐		25% of 700 km = ☐		25% of 200 kg = ☐
	25% of £400 = ☐		75% of 700 km = ☐		$12\frac{1}{2}$% of 200 kg = ☐
	$12\frac{1}{2}$% of £400 = ☐				$37\frac{1}{2}$% of 200 kg = ☐

5 Copy the grid and the shape on squared paper.

Draw the reflection of the shape in the mirror line.

Do this four times with shapes drawn with one vertex touching the mirror line.

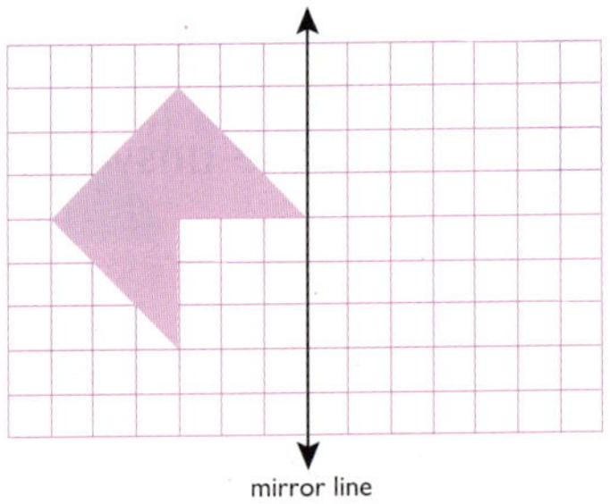

Practice 33b

1 Copy these and write the missing numbers.

1	☐ % of £400 = £100	2	☐ − 2·9 = 4·3	3	0·65 × ☐ = 1·3
4	☐ × 31 = 7812	5	☐ − 350 = 650	6	4 ÷ ☐ = 0·8
7	☐ ÷ 2 = 0·18	8	80% of ☐ = 2·4 cl	9	67 + (1386 ÷ ☐) = 100

2

1 Over 80% of the world's 6000 million population live north of the Equator. Approximately how many people live south of the Equator? What proportion of the world population is this?

2 The surface area of the Earth is about 510 million km^2. Saltwater covers nearly 70% of this. Approximately, how much of the Earth's surface is saltwater?

3 Approximately 7 million trees could be saved if only 10% of our waste paper and cardboard was recycled. About how many trees would be saved if we recycled all our waste paper and cardboard?

3

1 How many matches did Southstart play in the season?

2 In what percentage of matches did Southstart fail to score a goal?

3 In what percentage of matches did Southstart score more than one goal?

4 How many goals did they score in the season?

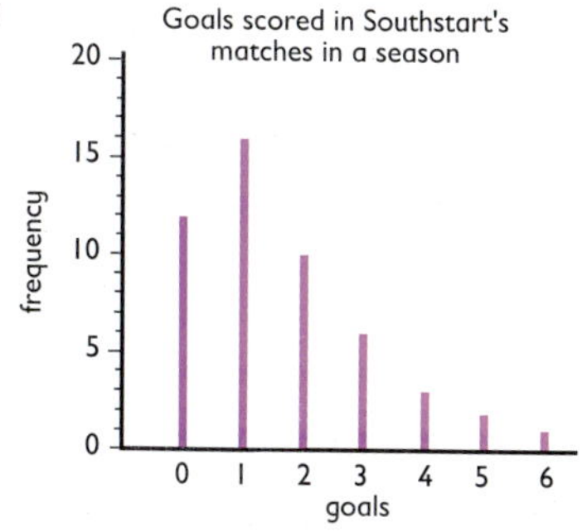

4 Copy the grid on squared paper. Draw the shape when it has been translated 5 squares up and 6 squares to the right.

On the same page, translate the original shape twice more:

1 7 down, 3 left 2 5 right, 8 up.

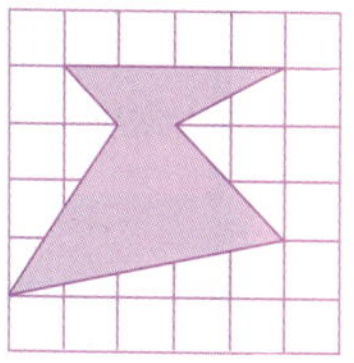

5 Copy the blank multiplication. Use all five digits from the box to complete the multiplication. Find the answer.

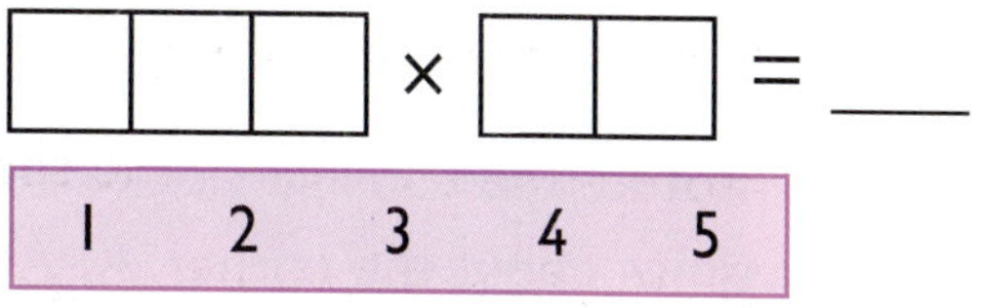

Do this three times.

Which arrangement of the five digits gives the smallest product?

Which arrangement of the five digits gives the largest product?

Practice 34a

1 Copy these and complete them.

1	$9 \div 10 =$ ____	2	$6{\cdot}55 \times 3 =$ ____	3	40% of 5 km
4	$\frac{11}{100}$ of 200 m	5	$10 - 2{\cdot}1 =$ ____	6	Sum of 0·41 and 0·5
7	$0{\cdot}35 \times 0{\cdot}5 =$ ____	8	75% of £2	9	$0{\cdot}67 - 0{\cdot}49 =$ ____

2

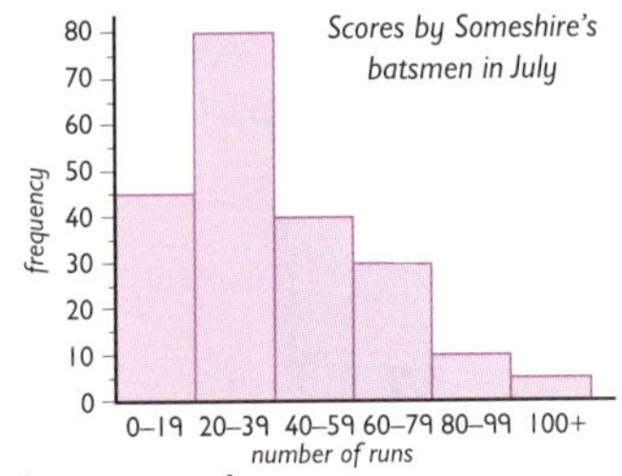

1 How many times did the batsmen score 40 to 59 runs?

2 How many batsmen's innings were there in July?

3 How many times was a century scored?

4 Kylie claims that 30 was the most frequent score. Explain why she is unlikely to be correct, based only on this graph.

3 Copy the table and the graph. You may find the graph helpful for completing the table.

gallons	litres
1	
	1
0·5	
	2·5
3·25	
	10

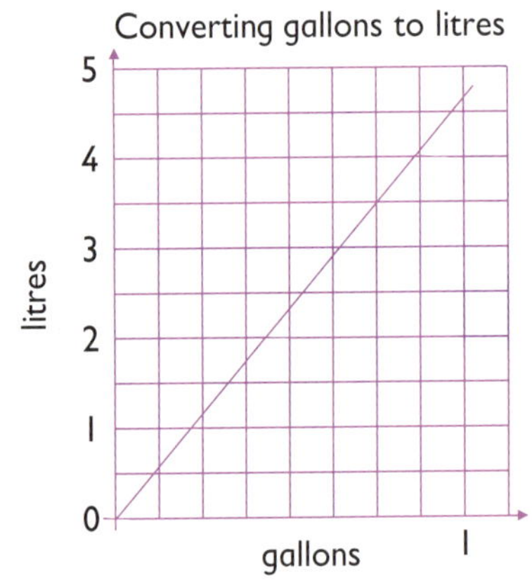

4

Times of 400 m in a 4 × 400 relay	
Name	Time in seconds
Tino	52·61
Adam	53·87
Euan	51·90
Dora	50·45

1 Who runs the fastest 400 metres?

2 How much slower was Tino than Euan?

3 How many metres was the relay?

4 What was the total time for the team for the whole race?

5 Why do you think Dora ran the last lap?

5 Copy the grid and the triangle.

Rotate the triangle clockwise 90 degrees three times about the corner A. After each rotation draw the triangle in its new position.

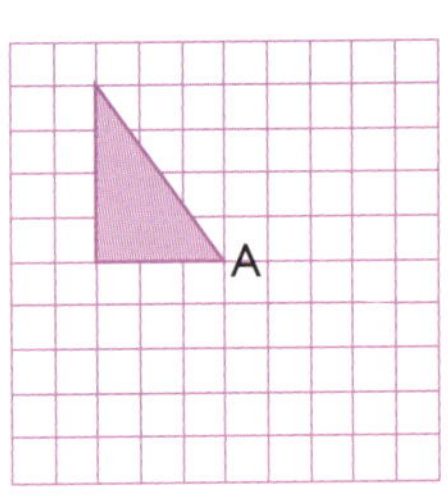

Do this three times for three shapes of your own.

Practice 34b

1 Copy these and write the missing numbers.

1 Half of ☐ = 0·25　　2 0·6 × ☐ = 3·6　　3 50% of ☐ = £4.50

4 3·61 + ☐ = 4　　5 6·6 – ☐ = 5·5　　6 ☐ % of 7 kg = 2·8 kg

7 $\frac{5}{6}$ of ☐ kg = 15 kg　　8 ☐ – 32 = 68　　9 3·88 × ☐ = 11·64

2 There are 32 children in Year 6.

1 What percentage of the class have a birthday between October and December?

2 Estimate the number of children who have a birthday in the second half of the year.

3 What fraction of the children have a birthday in the first three months of the year?

4 Jason says, 'Most children have their birthday in August.' Could he be correct? How do you know?

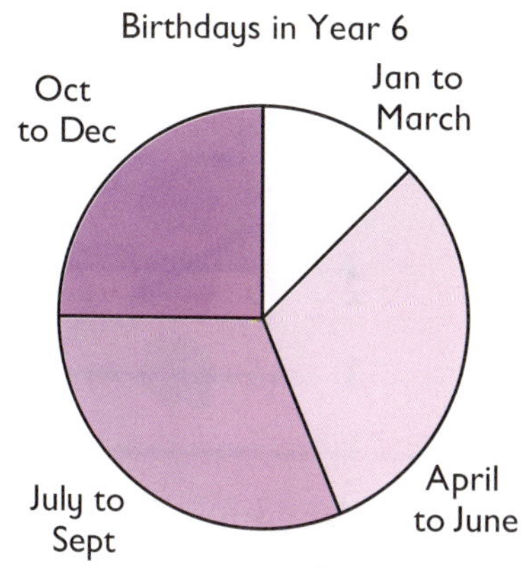

3 How many litres is in each container?

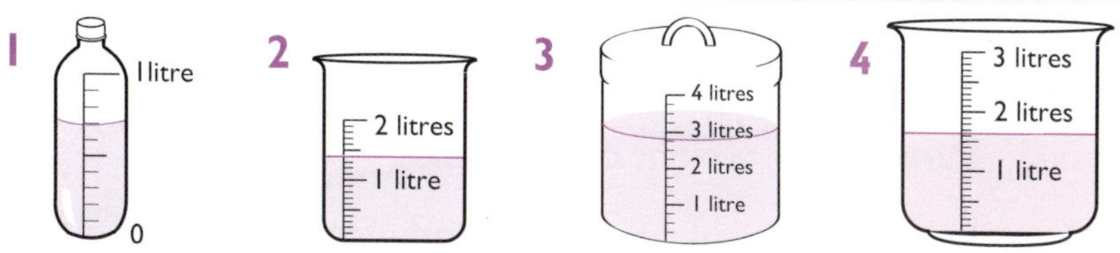

4 A plane, taking the long route, flies east around the world from London to New York, starting at 12:00 on 1st July. It stops at each city for 2 hours to refuel.

Construct a timetable which shows the local times and dates at each city when the plane arrives and departs.

City	Local time when 12:00 in London	Flight time from previous stop
London	12:00	
Amsterdam	13:00	1 hour
Singapore	20:00	10 hours
Sydney	22:00	12 hours
New York	07:00	11 hours

5 Copy the coordinate grid on squared paper.

Draw a non-rectangular quadrilateral in the first quadrant.

Draw the three reflections of the quadrilateral in each mirror line.

Do this again with a pentagon and then a hexagon.

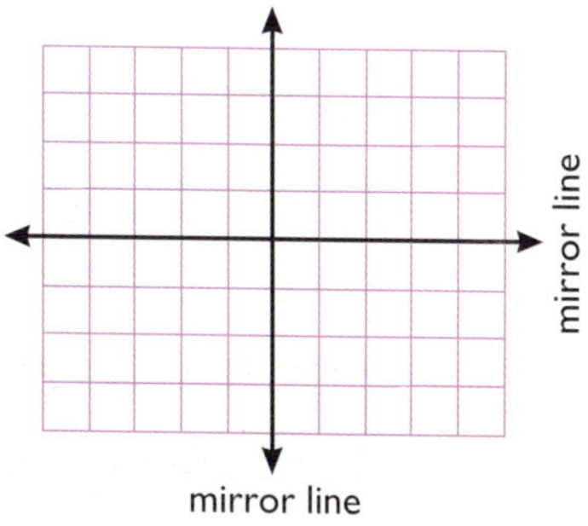

Practice 35a

1 Copy these and complete them.

1	2600 + 3900 = _____	2	8·6 + 0·9 = _____	3	7003 − 5890 = _____
4	3781 + 4926 = _____	5	20% of 15 m	6	3200 − 1700 = _____
7	9·2 − 0·9 = _____	8	2·31 × 10 = _____	9	6000 − 3888 = _____

2 Copy the calculations. Write the operations, +, −, × or ÷, that are hidden under the clouds.

1 (5 ☁ 4) ☁ (3 ☁ 2) = 45

2 (5 ☁ 4) ☁ (3 ☁ 2) = 20

3 (5 ☁ 4) ☁ (3 ☁ 2) = 54

3 When full, the fish tank and water together weigh 33 kilograms.

When half-full, the tank and water together weigh 18 kilograms.

What is the weight of the tank?

What is the weight of tank and water together when the tank is a quarter full?

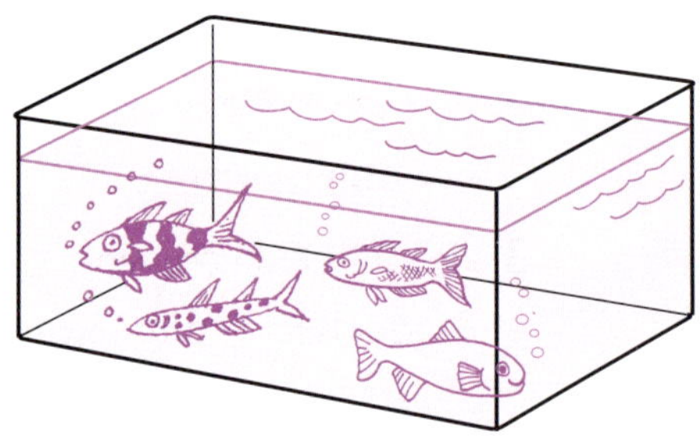

4 Copy the boxes and match equivalent amounts.

3 litres	0·3 litres	$\frac{3}{100}$ of a litre	3·3 litres	0·003 litres

300 ml	30 ml	3000 ml	3 ml	3300 ml

5 Copy the boxes and the incomplete numbers. Use all the digits 1 to 9 to complete the four numbers.

Find the sum and difference of each pair of numbers.

Do this four times.

	0	0	0

	9		

	0	0	0

	8		

Practice 35b

1 Copy these and write the missing numbers.

1	7004 − ☐ = 4008	2	☐ + 1·25 = 1·3	3	☐ + 3·6 = 32·7
4	☐ ÷ 100 = 0·02	5	10% of ☐ = 0·1 kg	6	☐ + 1700 = 3500
7	☐ × 4 = 2·8	8	9·7 − ☐ = 6·6	9	7500 − ☐ = 3700

2 Copy the incomplete statement. Choose two numbers from the box to complete the statement.

Do this six times.

☐ cl = ☐ l

0·13	130	30·1	310	
301	1·3	13	0·013	
1·03	103	3·1		

3 Rockford Primary School organizes a trip for its 235 children, 9 teachers and 40 adult helpers.

1 A coach seats 52 people. How many coaches are needed for everyone?

2 Ten children are ill and do not go on the trip. How many empty seats are there altogether?

3 The children who go on the trip are split into equal groups so that there is one teacher per group and at least four adult helpers. How many children are in each group? How many groups have five adult helpers?

4 Copy the grid onto squared paper.

1 The shape is moved: 4 right, 2 up and rotated 45° clockwise about its centre. Draw it in its new position.

2 Move the new shape: 4 down, 2 right and rotated 45° clockwise about its centre. Draw it in its new position.

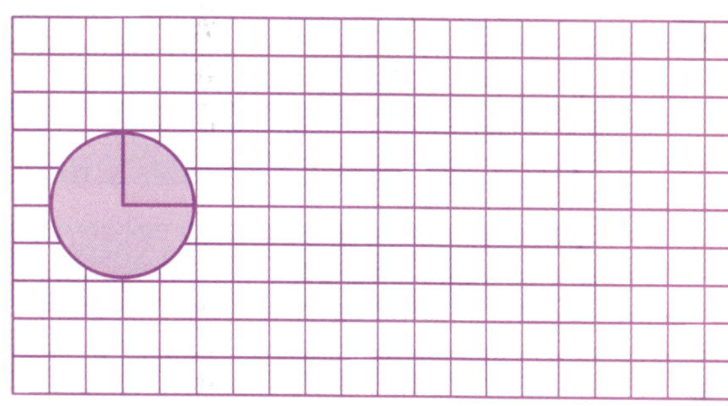

5 Copy the incomplete calculations. Choose digits from 1 to 9 to complete them. A digit may be used more than once.

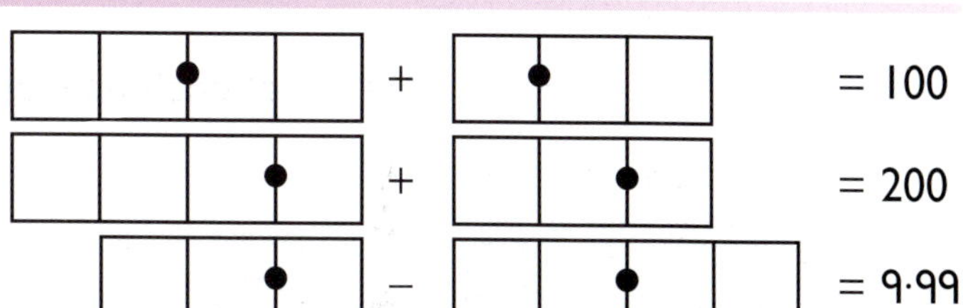

Practice 36a

1 Copy these and complete them.

1	Half of $0{\cdot}5$	2	$10 - 6{\cdot}6 =$ ____	3	$4000 - 1946 =$ ____
4	$0{\cdot}06 + 0{\cdot}4 =$ ____	5	$7{\cdot}8 - 1{\cdot}9 =$ ____	6	70% of 1 km
7	$0{\cdot}9 - 0{\cdot}47 =$ ____	8	$9000 - 4915 =$ ____	9	$5{\cdot}4 + 1{\cdot}9 =$ ____

2 Copy the incomplete prime factor diagrams.

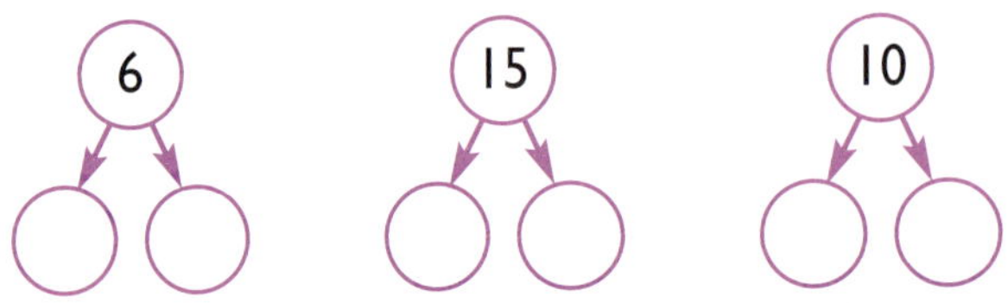

Draw diagrams for three more numbers that have only two prime factors.

Do this again for numbers which have only 3, 4 and 5 prime factors.

3

1. How many peaches are in 10 boxes?
2. Pat pays £3 for a box of peaches. How much must each peach be sold for so that he can make a profit of 10p on each peach?
3. A van can carry 210 boxes of peaches. How many journeys will the van have to make to transport 3000 boxes?

4 Write each of these relationships in symbols describing what each symbol represents.

1. The area of a rectangle is the product of its length and breadth.
2. The area of a square is the length of a side, squared.
3. Write a relationship showing how to find the area of a right-angled triangle.

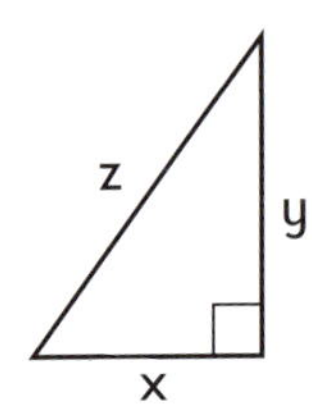

5 Copy the two blank decimal numbers. Use all of the digits in the box to complete the two numbers. Find the sum of the two numbers.

4	5	6	7	8	9

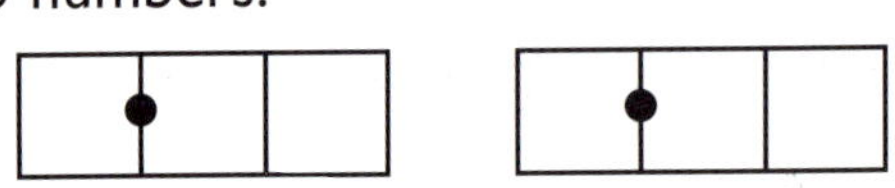

Find the arrangement of the six digits that gives the smallest sum possible.

Find the arrangement of the six digits that gives the largest sum possible.

Practice 36b

1 Copy these and write the missing numbers.

1	☐ + 2·1 = 8·9	2	☐ + 0·2 = 0·73	3	☐ − 1947 = 1053
4	100 − ☐ = 81	5	☐ − 3·17 = 37·45	6	☐ % of £6 = £4.50
7	0·47 − ☐ = 0·28	8	47 × ☐ = 329	9	☐ + 5·47 = 6

2 Copy and complete the diagram.

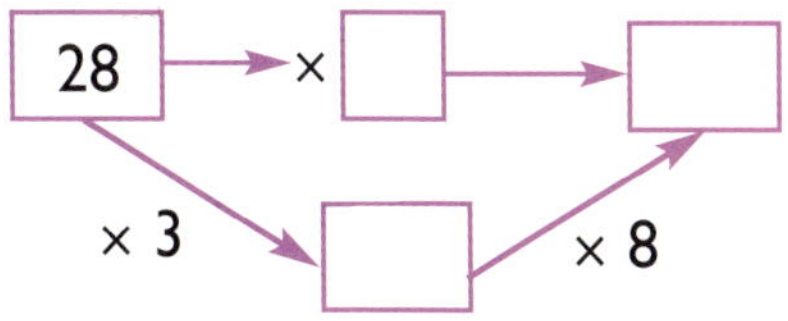

Write about how the diagram helps to find the answer to 28 × 24.

Draw diagrams to find the answers to:

33 × 24 23 × 32 41 × 28

3

1 When Newchester Rovers play Chelsfield the ground is full. How much in total do the spectators pay?

2 In the game against Welford there were 4159 seats empty in the East Stand. How much did those in the East Stand pay for that match altogether?

3 What is the mean cost of a seat?

Seats at Newchester Rovers

	number of seats	cost of a seat
West Stand	9384	£20
East Stand	15 078	£25
North Stand	6115	£12.50
South Stand	8263	£17.50

4 These numbers are palindromes. What is special about numbers which are palindromes?

22 131 4994 17271

Find all the palindromes between 1 and 1000.

5 Copy the incomplete sequence. Make up a rule for the sequence and find the next five numbers.

1 3 ☐ ☐ ☐ ☐ ☐

Do this again three times using a different rule each time.